P9-CAL-683

GAME PLAN

THE GAME INVENTOR'S HANDBOOK

STEPHEN PEEK

BETTERWAY PUBLICATIONS, INC.
WHITE HALL, VIRGINIA

Published by Betterway Publications, Inc.
Box 8561
White Hall, VA

Cover design and illustrations by Cynthia Sims Kirkland
Typesetting by TechType

Library of Congress Cataloging-in-Publication Data

Peek, Stephen
    Gameplan: the game inventor's handbook/Stephen Peek
        p. cm
    Includes index.
    ISBN 0-932620-85-X (pbk.) : $9.95
    1. Games--Marketing.   I. Title.
  HD9993.G352P44 1987
  794' .068--dc 19   87-15921
                                       CIP

Printed in the United States of America
0 9 8 7 6 5 4 3 2 1

PREFACE

I have a story to tell you. It goes like this....

In the year 1454, in the town of Mainz, Germany, Johann Gutenberg had just finished binding his first bible. Ecstatic, he sought an audience with the local baron, from whom he sought financial assistance. With tremendous pride, he delivered the fruits of his lifetime of labor into the hands of this elegantly dressed gentleman. The baron opened the book and casually thumbed through its beautifully printed pages. He closed it, placed it on the desk before him and, with his right index finger, thoughtfully tapped the massive volume. "Herr Gutenberg, this is marvelous! Truly a wonder!," he exclaimed. "But, you see, I've got a great idea for a game, and..."

The rest, as they say, is history. I'm sure the baron convinced poor, trusting Johann to go into partnership on a board game venture. And I'm pretty sure they went to work immediately printing the baron's newly invented game, whatever it was, because the next year Mr. Gutenberg went bust and was forced to sell his press. It just goes to show you; when in doubt, stick with bibles.

This isn't exactly a cheery note on which to start a book about getting into the board game business. The painful truth is that out of an estimated three to four thousand games that enter the market every year, only a scant handful can expect to be found on retailers' shelves two years later. The rest are doomed to gather dust in warehouses, basements and garages. In some cases, the games won't even remain on the market long enough to have a chance of becoming moneymakers.

GAME MARKETING   Marketing games is very different from selling books or movies – exactly the opposite, in fact. When a new book or movie is released there's a great deal of hype and hoopla. Advertising space is bought in newspapers, in magazines and on radio and television. Six to eight weeks later the publisher or film producer not only knows whether he has a winner: he can also gauge how big a winner it will be and act accordingly. This pattern does not hold true for games.

Word of Mouth is the Key

The fact is that virtually every game ever made was on the market for at least four years before anybody had an inkling that it would be a hit. The reason: a game's popularity builds – or loses – momentum by word-of-mouth. Someone plays a game at a friend's place. If he likes it, he buys it to play with someone else, and so forth. It's a slow type of advertising but, if the product is a good one, it will hold up well under this system.

Several major companies have tried to shorten this tedious process by spending huge amounts of money promoting games they felt would be winners. One company spent nearly $25 million advertising a new game in its first year. The advertising bought a lot of shelf space in stores (more about this later), but the game grossed less than $18 million. While this game is still on the market today, it's not one people talk about – or buy – very much.

This all sounds rather negative and, admittedly, it is. If you are serious about getting a game into print, however, you should be aware of the pitfalls before you start. Many people tend to skim over these details and concentrate only on visions of wealth, fame and glory. An important first step is to understand one's motivations, to determine exactly why you, and others, want to create games.

Game companies – those engaged in the design, manufacture and distribution of games – do it for one reason and that is, obviously, to make money. Most individuals who invent games think they are doing it for the money also, but this isn't the case. The real reason is ego: everybody wants a chance to be a big fish in the pond. By publishing a game you join a small, elite group of people who have overcome anxieties about personal failure and financial loss, who have thrown caution to the winds in an effort to fulfill a dream. Realistically, how many will make it big? After nearly fourteen years in the game business I have met, corresponded with, spoken to or heard from literally thousands of people who had invented a game they wanted to publish. Of these, I can think of at least three who have become wealthy from their efforts. A number of others have achieved some success, made some money, but only those three, to my knowledge, have really hit it big.

Since I am a medium-sized fish in the modest gaming pool, I have a constant stream of people coming to me seeking advice on how to get published. It's a little like being a doctor. As soon as someone discovers your profession they begin talking about their pains – or, in my case, games. It seems nearly everyone I meet has designed a really great game that, if published, would make a fortune. Many of these people drift away after listening to my negative lectures. Only a few die-hards remain, stubbornly insisting they are going to get their names into print. Sometimes I help them and sometimes I don't.

In 1980, a recently widowed lady in her late sixties came to me. She and her husband had bred dogs all their lives and she had devised a game based on dog shows. She was prepared to spend nearly all her meager inheritance, money she would need later in life for a decent retirement. I thought breeders and other dog show devotees might find the game somewhat interesting, though a bit dull perhaps. The biggest problem, I felt, was that the game would have such a limited market there would be little point in producing it for profit. Therefore, I tried to convince the lady not to do it at all. Failing this, I hoped to talk her into making only a thousand copies as a test run. I reasoned that her cost per unit would be astronomical but it would be a way she could 'test' the product without gambling on her future security.

Determination is Essential

She refused to listen to me. She insisted on having 10,000 copies finished and delivered within three months. I told her I didn't think she should do the game and I would not help her. Then I recommended some printers and fabricators I knew to be honest and wished her luck. She had her ten thousand games made and hit the dog show circuit to market them. Four years later, as far as I know, she still had eight thousand games filling the garage and two bedrooms of her home. The point of this story is not to heap another negative on a growing pile, but to stress that if you are serious about doing a game, you absolutely must share a trait with the lady dog breeder – determination. (Of course, doing a little test marketing before "taking the plunge" is not a bad trait to have either.) If you don't have determination, forget the whole thing because you'll be wasting time and money.

Okay, let's assume you are serious and intend to let nothing stand in your way. First, permit yourself to run through this little test below. Be honest in answering now!

THE PROSPECTIVE GAME CREATOR'S NO-WIN QUIZ

1. Just suppose no game publisher will buy your game and you are forced to publish it yourself. Regardless of how you go about it, your game is going to cost between ten and twenty thousand dollars for a limited test run. Can you afford to lose this much money?

2. Are you prepared to work at marketing the game for a minimum of four years, incurring substantial expenses in addition to the cost of printing the game, to determine if it will become a successful money maker?

3. Are you willing to work nights and weekends – in addition to your regular full-time occupation – filling orders, invoicing accounts, setting up and maintaining a set of books, designing and placing advertisements, attending expensive trade exhibits and consumer shows? Are you willing to do all this – and much more – in addition to lying awake at night worrying about your investment?

4. Are you willing to do all these things, knowing the odds are heavily against you and at best you'll probably break even?

5. Are you willing to endure all this just for a big stake in a small pond?

If you answered NO to any of these questions, you may be better off sticking to bibles. If you are unsure about taking a gamble but can't chuck the idea altogether, my advice is to go to Las Vegas, plunk down ten thousand dollars on the color red at the roulette table and take your chances there. The end will come a lot quicker and be a lot less painful. However, if you answered YES to all the questions, bless your heart: it looks as though you're ready to dive into the murky waters of the gaming pond. So, get ready for the wildest ride of your life. All forewarnings aside, it may just be the most rewarding adventure you'll ever have.

Once you make the decision to go ahead with your game, you should know that the odds are against your selling it to an existing game company. While the next section tells how to go about approaching game publishers, the bulk of this book is written under the assumption that you are so bull-headed and stubborn that no matter what, you're determined to get this game published, even if it means having to pay to do it yourself.

CONTENTS

INTRODUCTION: A HISTORY OF GAMES

CHESS Invented 4000 Years Ago

The history of games is tied to Man in the same way Man's history is connected to conflict. It's interesting to know that *HOUNDS AND JACKALS*, the game beautiful, young Nefertiti and wise old Rameses played in the movie, "The Ten Commandments", was a real game, or to learn chess, which some believed was invented in Europe around the middle of the Dark Ages, probably dates back to China, 2,000 B.C.. It's intriguing to learn artifacts from long deceased civilizations, far predating written history, clearly demonstrate the presence of games in the most primitive of societies; and in the nothing-ever-changes-department, to discover Roman soldiers, faced with the tedium of duty in foreign lands, shot an ancient form of *CRAPS* for the robe of Jesus.

Games are Part of Man's Social Evolution

All this is interesting to a point . If it continued much further it would cease to be interesting and become a string of facts, names and dates like so much history. Fortunately for the easily bored, much of gaming's past does in fact pre-date written history and is subject to much speculation. For example there are at least seven versions recounting the origin of *GO*, Japan's national game, and even more stories about the invention of chess. What may be fascinating is a comparison of the development of games along with the social evolution of Man.

War: a Theme of Games for Centuries

In the beginning it's almost certain games were of the physical sort. Who could throw the farthest and straightest, run the fastest, hit the hardest – games designed to improve survival odds. Then, when man discovered leisure time, sometime during the Neolithic era, games began to assume the qualities of mans greatest endeavor –

war; organized running and hitting -- all designed to improve an individual's chance of survival. Chess, not even so abstractly, certainly has its roots in warfare, as do *CHECKERS* and *GO*. War remains the dominant theme in games for many centuries and naturally so. War, even into are own era, remains the greatest undertaking of mankind. The connection between war and gaming is so close that in Prussia in 1811, during one of those rare momentary respites when politicians were not bandying swords over national property lines, Baron von Reisswitz and his son took the abstract pieces off the chess board and replaced them with cannon, infantry, and cavalry to turn an intellectual pastime into a training tool designed to increase the survival odds.

But war is only one path. Man has other conflicts in his checkered history and games seem naturally to follow conflict. Sometime during the Middle Ages there was a amazing invention. Before the invention wealth could only be measured in precious metals, jewels, land, slaves and other real assets. Most of the real assets were held by nobility, who unleashed legions of headbashers to collect huge portions of precious metals obtained by common folk from selling potatoes and such. The wealth was pretty much controlled by nobility and one was either born to nobility or not. Consequently, very little creativity was expended toward raising wealth – there was only so much of it, the nobility had it, and if a nobleman wanted to increase his own he had only to unleash more headbashers than the lord in the castle next door and take his wealth. Since headbashers cost almost as much as a decent horse, nobles tend not to risk them against opposing headbashers very often. So things remained pretty much the same until two things happened – the invention of paper money and the ability to put this paper representation of real assets into financial institutes where they could be recorded, traded, borrowed against, loaned out at interest and impounded by irate nobleman who sensed the decentralization of their power base. It takes more than headbashing to stop a great idea and the financial institutes flourished, creating the next conflict for gaming –the concept of getting rich.

Nothing has spawned more games than the hunt for wealth . Real estate, stock market, gambling, business – even educational games, use as their central lure the prospect of accumulating vast amounts of money. When it comes to getting rich, nothing is sacred. There are games dealing with selling dope, getting into heaven, even entering politics and wars and profit.

**More Complex
Games Reflect
Societal Changes**

Games have become even more sophisticated in much the same manner as Man. What was once, long ago, a black and white, good versus evil world is now a world full of gray areas. Gaming, being an integral part of humanity, has followed suit, changing once simple abstract rules into complex collections of redundant verbiage intended to simulate incredibly intricate social patterns and events.

Where will it end? No one knows, not with any confidence anyway. Every year there are those who gamble there real wealth on a idea for a game which they are sure will catch the fancy of the current generation and turn them, the game entrepreneurs, into 20th century nobility.

But one thing is certain. Although there is some prosperity derived from fad games, the games which feed on our most basic conflicts and desires are the ones which will become the phenomenal successes, the ones that are apt to last as long as chess and the other classics.

What will they be like, those super successes? I'm convinced they will be artificial intelligence computer programs combined with the powerful visual effects, displayed in 3-D surroundings designed to increase the odds of survival.

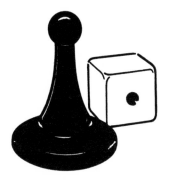

PUBLISHER, WILL YOU BUY?

Every dream cannot come true. Selling your game to a game publisher is desirable, but it is an unlikely accomplishment for the first-time game inventor.

PITCHING THE BIG LEAGUES

Let's face it: every game designer's dream is to sell a game to one of the major companies and have it become the next MONOPOLY. However, the odds against this happening are incredibly steep. Consider how many new games come out every year and then consider that a phenomenon like MONOPOLY or TRIVIAL PURSUIT occurs maybe once every twenty to thirty years. Add to that scenario the difficulty of convincing a major company to even look at a new game and the whole ballgame begins to look like a "no win" situation. But ...it's not impossible.

Before I started this book I mailed a letter of inquiry to the fifty largest board game companies in the United States. I already knew what they were going to say, but I wanted it to be official. My letter stated right off that I did not have a game to show them. I then explained that I was writing this book and that I would appreciate their sending me a statement of their official policy regarding outside submissions.

Thirty-seven of the companies did not even bother to reply. The rest, with one exception, sent back a printed rejection letter stating flatly, under no circumstances, would the firm examine or consider a game from an outside source. The one exception was a form letter with a hand written note scribbled on it inviting me to call, under the proviso that I would not mention the name of the individual or his firm in this book.

After speaking with this game world's "deep throat" I was able to confirm the following: officially – on the record – his firm's policy was the same as all the others. In short, save your postage. Unofficially, as far as "deep throat" was aware, there are three ways to to get a major company to even consider looking at an outsider's game.

TRY THIS GAME PLAN

The first possibility: if you find your game is batting .750 in minor league markets and getting good press in general, try offering it to the larger game companies. TRIVIAL PURSUIT, for example, had been out for a couple of years in Canada, doing very well there and reasonably well here in the United States (where it was selling for forty dollars) when it attracted the attention of Selchow & Righter (the Scrabble people). They then obtained the rights to manufacture and sell it. The rest is history.

An alternative suggestion: become an established game inventor, with one or more games under your belt. This, naturally, will give you an "in" when making future proposals to game companies. Of course, this also creates the Catch-22 situation of how to get that experience when no one will give you a job in the first place.

Producing Your Own Game

This brings us to your third possibility: Produce your own game. Market it with all the determination and enthusiasm you can muster. Then, when it has become moderately successful, submit a letter of inquiry to the company you've targeted. With the letter, include a marketing brief detailing the history of the game's sales, including where it sold, retailers who sell it and how much money has been spent to establish a foothold in the market. This method is your most practical shot at getting a large game company to look at your work. If it's not possible, either for lack of funds, time or energy, there's still one avenue open.

Produce the game as cheaply as possible, even if it means as few as 100 copies at a quick copy printer. Make certain, however, to include 'TM' by the title and the official copyright line on the box. Run a classified ad in the newspapers and beg any retailers you know to put the game in their outlets on a consignment basis. Then, dig in and deluge the game companies with letters and phone calls. Visit them personally if possible. Whatever you do, be persistent! Make it clear that the game has already been produced, regardless of the quality. The odds are still very much against success but at least there's a chance someone will relent, show some compassion, and look at your work.

DO PUBLISHERS HAVE TO BE SO TOUGH?

Why do major companies resist looking at outside submissions? Reasons can vary from firm to firm, but the three most common are legal expenses, time and marketing.

No one likes to be sued. It's an unpleasant, ulcer-inducing experience that can cost thousands of dollars – even if you win. Since game companies always have a backlog of games in various stages of design and production, they have to be extremely careful when considering outside submissions. They may decide to reject a game because it is similar to one already in development. When their own game hits the market, the freelance designer might see it, think the company has stolen his idea and get his attorney-cum-brother-in-law to file suit. Don't shake your head: it's a story that's been repeated over and over. Even if the company wins the suit, which they usually do (because of peculiar copyright laws governing board games) there's still the matter of tens of thousands of dollars in legal fees.

Time is another obstacle. If a company the size of Parker Brothers looked at every game that arrived in their morning's mail, they'd need two or three full time game analysts to even begin to evaluate just the few proposals that showed promise.

Your Game Has to Fit Their Plans

The third reason for resistance – marketing – may seem the strangest of all. Most major firms do employ a game designing staff, but you'd be surprised at how small these staffs are. The few people who manage to land these jobs don't get to sit around in an idyllic world dreaming up games. In many cases, it's the marketing department that decides the subject and style of the projects. They do a thorough study, then send a memo to the design department advising the inventors of the needed requirements. The intention might be to devise a game about three cartoon characters in a giant washing machine. It might have to be for eight year olds, inoffensive to the American Indian, playable in seven to fifteen minutes and packaged so that it can sell for $3.99 – which comes down to a small game board, a box, one die and six playing pieces. What all this means, of course, is that even if a company does agree to look at a free lance game, if it doesn't click with current marketing plans, it's out – no matter how good it is.

Looking at it from the other side, then, there is a legitimate rationale underpinning the large companies' aversion to outside submissions. But what about the not-so-major companies? There are many more of them.

HOW ABOUT THE SMALL AND MEDIUM-SIZE GAME PRODUCERS?

Small-to-medium-sized companies sometimes will accept a submission if the game seems interesting and fits the parameters of their market. But, watch out! These companies generally don't have the money to pay advances, nor the necessity. Designers need them a lot more than they need designers. They may do things like market less than five thousand copies of a game as a test. What this means for you is that even if the game does catch on, the chances are your royalties won't buy you a new car every fifth year. What if you succeed in selling your game to a publisher? Well, once you do, it belongs to whoever bought it, body and soul. Sure, there's a royalty agreement, but what happens if the game attracts the attention of a major company and the smaller company sells it to them? Chances are, if you signed a fairly standard contract, you'll get royalties based on what the company receives from the resale, which means they wind up with 90% or better and you're left trying to figure out what happened.

RULES FOR SUBMITTING GAMES

If you want to have any chance of getting companies to look at your game, follow this advice ...

1. Never, under any circumstances, send a game until a company asks for it. If they do, they'll usually require a signed release exempting them from blame for any conceivable event. Unsolicited games, or the use of certified mail for routine inquiries, will simply make people mad.

2. If the game has been produced in any form and is to be submitted as such, be sure to have the legal copyright line imprinted on the box, board, rules and any other printed matter. Check with an attorney or the U.S. Copyright Office for details.

3. When sending a letter of inquiry, keep it brief and to the point, but include the following: whether you have sold other games to other companies; the subject of the game you are submitting;

the age range, length of playing time, length of rules (a word count); a list of components with a line saying you have examined games produced by this particular company and feel the game falls within their standard component range. A separate enclosure should have a thorough marketing summary sheet of the game's sales record and copies of ads and major coverage. All this should be typed neatly, double spaced on a sheet containing your name, address and telephone number. Do not send a form letter or a photocopy. And many companies and individuals find copy produced on a dot matrix printer difficult to read.

4. If at all possible obtain the name of the person who decides which games will be produced, and use it on all correspondence.

5. If you know anyone who is in any way associated with the toy and game industry on a national level, try to enlist their assistance to help you get a foot in the door.

6. Keep hammering! You may have to send dozens of letters and make scores of phone calls just to get someone to talk to you. Most people don't like to say NO. Since their company policy requires them to say it so often, they probably prefer not to get involved at all with anyone making an unsolicited game submission.

MY IRISH FRIEND

I have a friend I've never met, at least not face to face. His name is Herbie Brennan. Herbie and I have corresponded and chatted over the phone for years. Someday I hope to travel to his 200 year old home in the Emerald Island share a bottle of fine Irish whiskey with him. He's primarily a writer with twenty or so books to his credit, ranging from management guides to fantasy novels. He's also a business consultant, a partner in a direct marketing firm, an ex-advertising agency executive, an astrologer, acupuncturist, herbalist and just about every other kind of "ist" there is. I am telling you about him because he's a game inventor who's been fortunate enough and smart enough to sell his games to other companies. I've imposed on our friendship to ask him, as an experienced invention/ideas marketeer, to share his thoughts on selling a game to a publisher. The following pages are his contribution to your success in the game industry.

* * * * * *

THE ROAD TO FAME AND FORTUNE

Yessir, there are publishers out there - people who will take your idea, package it, market it and promote it all at their own expense. As the game sells, they will pay you money in the form of royalties; in some instances, they may even be persuaded to pay you money in the form of an advance, before your game ever gets into the stores. It's an awful lot easier and much less risky than marketing your own game, however much you may learn in the following pages. But it has one drawback. Finding a publisher for that first game you have invented is like finding truffles in a French forest - you know the damn things are there all right, but you have to root around like crazy to unearth even one.

Just how difficult it is to find a publisher for a first game is underscored by the research Steve did before he started this book. He received only thirteen responses to fifty inquiries mailed to the largest board game companies – and he wasn't even asking anyone to look at a game.

The truth is that really big game companies are unlikely to touch you with a ten-foot pole. The small-to-medium-sized publishers might be interested in your wares, but your chances of a smash-hit marketing success with them are much less than with a huge publisher because small companies don't have the same distribution network or anything like the promotional budget.

If your game is a winner, however, and if it has that compulsive, addictive quality that keeps players coming back for more, then it's going to claw a way up through the marketplace with a little bit of luck and a reasonable amount of business expertise. Your biggest problem – interesting a publisher – will hinge on a secondary problem of defining the product you are marketing with utmost clarity.

Let's take that second problem first. Since games are invented in stages, you might simply come up with a brilliant idea and leave it at that, or you might work the idea through into a detailed concept. Maybe you'll go so far as to do sample design and artwork, in order to have a full-scale, professional-looking prototype to tuck under your arm. You may have already produced and marketed your own game, and now wish to try to interest a publisher in taking the ball and running with it further than you think you can on your own. Selling a publisher on your product requires a number of different techniques, depending upon the stage in your game's development at which you choose to make your move.

THE PERILS OF IDEAS

There is a market for ideas. It is a risky and difficult market, and unlikely to make you wealthy, but it does exist. To get anywhere at all, you'll need to hold two strong cards for openers – the ideas themselves and the ability to express them persuasively. Then you'll need patience, perseverance, a thick skin, a hard nose, and a good lawyer.

This is a market rich in legal quicksand, for copyright protection of an idea (as opposed to the expression of that idea) is nearly impossible to establish. The net result: when you try to sell an idea, you

run a very real risk of having it stolen, with no legal redress whatsoever. For this reason you'll find that everybody, but everybody, in
the ideas market is a raving paranoid. But try it anyway. You might
even enjoy it. Some people wrestle alligators for a living.

The strangest thing is that the most paranoid people of all will be
the people to whom you will have to offer your ideas. The very ones
you should fear may take your vision and run are the ones most dis-
turbed by the fact that your "baby" doesn't have any clear cut legal
protection.

**Why Is Everyone
So Paranoid?**   Ideas float freely in the air, waiting to be picked like fruit. You can
bet that the most ingenious notion you have ever had will be shared
by someone, somewhere. Since the world is a mighty big place, the
emergence of the same idea in different locations rarely creates conflicts, indeed often fails even to attract notice. Take the theory of
evolution, for instance. It was a pretty far-out notion when it occurred to Darwin, but not so far out that Wallace didn't think of it at
the same time. There was no question of collusion; history simply
attests that these two great scientists somehow achieved a more or
less identical thought quite independently. When it happens that
two versions of the same idea come into headlong collision,
however, people tend to reach for their attorneys the same way
Wild Bill Hickok used to reach for his gun.

Put yourself in the position of the president of a big company. You
have your own research and development team, funded by a multi-
million dollar budget. This team comes up with potential new
products all the time. Most of these fail to pass a limited market test;
nonetheless, the team continues to brainstorm and conceive. Right
now they're working on the greatest game since ... In the midst of
these continuing creative explosions, your secretary brings you the
morning's mail. In the pile is a letter from a 44-year-old school-
teacher in Columbus, Ohio outlining substantially the same hot idea
your R&D team is currently developing. The teacher thinks it's a
good notion and wants you to make her an offer.

You spot problems right away. You aren't about to waste company
money paying for an idea your own team already hit upon. At the
same time, you can see that the teacher isn't going to believe you

when you tell her she's too late. The minute your letter reaches her, stating your men had the idea first, she's going to sue. She may not win the suit, but that doesn't matter. The very fact that she mounts a legal action will cost you time and money, and bring you bad publicity. It's a no-win situation no matter the final judgment.

Game Submissions Are Often Returned Unopened

It's such a no-win situation that major corporations (inside and out of the game industry) just won't sit still for it. Submissions are returned unopened, if possible, or unread beyond the point where it becomes obvious you're about to tell them your idea.

Some corporations, however, don't go quite that far. Their executives harbor the distant hope that somewhere out there somebody might just have an idea that will make money. They want to consider outside submissions, but they don't want to end up in a legal mess, so they implement a killer policy – killer, that is, from the standpoint of the "outside" game inventor. The first step in this strategy is to announce that no ideas will be considered unless preceded by a letter requesting permission to submit the idea. The second step is for the company to send you a legally binding contract to sign.

This contract, when it arrives, has nothing at all to do with your idea (which, of course, you haven't submitted yet). Instead, it is a document absolutely freeing the corporation from any responsibility whatsoever for what they may do with your idea when you do submit it. It's a document attesting to your relinquishment of all rights to your idea, and it pledges to you take no legal action against the corporation even if they steal it. In short, it's a document that wipes out every legal right you have, thus placing you in the position of absolute trust vis a vis the corporation.

Believe it or not, I have signed such documents. I didn't like it, but I couldn't see any viable options. At the same time, I am pleased to report I have never been cheated by a corporation. It's sort of like the mechanism a dog will use when he gets into a fight that's too much for him. He'll roll over submissively and offer his throat ... at which point the big dog savaging him usually loses interest and backs off.

I'm not advocating that you sign every such killer contract that comes your way. What I am saying is that if you are in the ideas market you have to be realistic and see that the other fellow has his problems too. If the company issuing the contract is well established and respectable, then the chances are they are only being cautious and are not trying to steal your brilliant notion. Contracts of this type issued by an unknown corporation, or one with a reputation for sharp practices, however, should be dumped in the garbage.

When To Sign a Contract What it all comes down to is this: if you can find a corporation that will consider your idea without forcing you to sign the sort of contract Faust made with Mephistopheles, count yourself lucky and send them the idea. If an established company requires you to sign, do so. The chances are you will come out with a whole skin, but you should also be aware that even if they don't steal your idea, you have given them an unquestionable edge when it comes to working out the payment agreement. In effect, legally they can pay you anything they want – or nothing at all. Most corporations are fair when it comes to payment, but none are all that fair. You're going to be a bit disappointed in the deal you get eventually.

If a shady company insists you sign the contract, don't. You may find someone better, more reliable, if you keep looking. Or you may eventually find yourself in a position to market the idea yourself.

* * * * *

DECIDING ON YOUR PRESENTATION Now it's time to take a long hard look at your game and the form in which to present it. In some industries, the most basic idea is worth money in its own right. Several years ago I acted as agent for a British inventor who came up with a very interesting notion for manufacturers of audio cassette tapes. At that time, cassette manufacturers used plain leader tapes. The inventor's bright idea was to replace this leader with tape that cleaned the recording head: a simple concept and one that I thought was potentially marketable.

As things turned out, it earned no money for the inventor and no commission for me. The company to which the idea was submitted declined to buy it on the grounds that autocleaning sound tapes would not have public appeal, and such tapes would interfere with their sales of special headcleaning cassettes.

In marketing terms the company was wrong on the first point and right on the second. Autocleaning tapes are now on the market and their added value aspect has made them popular with cassette users. They are so popular, in fact, that the profits from increased sales far outweigh the losses experienced in the area of specialized headcleaning cassettes.

None of this was of any use to the British inventor, however. While we were still hawking the idea around, an overseas company introduced it commercially. There was no question of theft. As I said earlier, good ideas float about in the air. To make money from them, you have to be not just imaginative but quick and lucky as well.

An idea as simple as this might have potential in some fields but, I regret to report, the game industry is not one of them. Game publishers have good ideas coming out of their ears and most of them have been used in some form or another. What they want, if anything at all, is a developed proposal. They believe, quite rightly in my opinion, that just about every worthwhile idea has been tried in some form or another. The crucial factor for success is the specific implementation.

When it comes to boxed games the presentation of your idea has to be pretty thorough. You have to have the rules in final form and give a very clear indication of how the board should look, what sort of pieces your game requires and so on. A brief synopsis is useless. In this area, you are no longer really marketing a rough idea. To all intents and purposes you are creating a prototype of your new game.

There is, however, one sector where underdeveloped ideas are still welcome and that is the volatile home computer game industry.

A BYTE INTO THE SOFTWARE MARKET

In the past couple of years computer games have enjoyed an upsurge in popularity so great that they have made many an entrepreneur quite wealthy. Consequently, more and more hopeful companies are attracted to this market, producing a flood of lookalike, me-too software. As the competition heightens, software houses become increasingly desperate for programs which will help them capture large chunks of the market.

Game Design and Programming Skill Is Essential

Such corporations have a fundamental problem. The creation of a computer game requires two very separate skills – the ability to program and the ability to design a worthwhile game. Rare is the individual endowed with both these skills, so many software corporations are willing -- and some actually anxious -- to listen to computer game ideas, even if it's obvious that you can't tell a PEEK from a POKE. This can be a lucrative market bearing in mind that there are a few caveats.

Just as in the board game market, larger software houses have their own creative departments and are much less interested in outside submissions (in idea form) than their smaller competitors. Also, the sad truth is that the software industry has more cowboys in it than Boot Hill, more crapshooters than in Las Vegas and Atlantic City combined. You need to take special care to pick a small company with some track record, not one that opened its doors yesterday and may well close them again tomorrow.

Selecting a reputable target company in this sector is far from easy, but there are some helpful guidelines. You might, for example, study their advertising. Cheap, amateurish advertising indicates a cheap, amateurish company. Limited advertising suggests a company that's short on capital. Both are bad news for you as a prospective ideas marketeer. Consequently, it's important to look at a sample of the company's products. There's a great deal of rubbish software on the market and if standards are low, you are well advised to avoid that particular company.

The final consideration is how much the company will promise you for your idea. This is the trickiest part of all because – paradoxically – the higher the offer, the less likely it is that you are getting a sound deal.

I have in my files a collection of bizarre advertisements from a variety of software houses offering rewards of $50,000 plus for game programs and program ideas. Some promise royalties as high as 35%. It may sound like a dream come true, but chances are it isn't. There's no such thing as a free lunch. Even in the overpriced software market you need a lot of sales to generate $50,000, plus a decent profit for the software house itself. Unless your idea is sufficiently gripping to generate mass sales, you won't get high rewards, no matter how fervently they have been promised. Software corporations are not in the charity business. The big royalties they may promise are always tempting, but there is a level at which they become unrealistic to everybody, and the laws of marketing must take over. Like any other product, a game is commercially successful only if its income exceeds the expenditure required to produce and market it; a 35% royalty calculated retail or wholesale will overbalance every marketing equation I've ever seen.

Computer Game Packaging   Assuming you've managed to avoid the cowboys and crapshooters and have found a software house anxious to consider your game ideas, there is still the question of packaging – an element of your presentation that may be as important as the product itself.. Even the best ideas require good packaging if they are to sell – which is another way of saying you should take the time and trouble to present properly. Let's look at a concrete example of ideas presentation:

About two years ago or so, while suffering from exhaustion caused by playing SPACE INVADERS, I decided it would be fun to have my own computer game on the market. The hitch was that I had almost no idea how to program a computer. This threw me back to creating and selling a game program idea. There was no way I could even hack together a rough simulation of how it would look on a screen so I had to package it in such a way as to appeal to a software house.

My basic idea arose out of market analysis. It was obvious at the time that the big-selling home computer games were of the shoot 'em up, arcade variety. It was also fairly obvious to me that the market for arcade games was overcrowded and the boom in sales could not last forever.

A closer look at the situation yielded more insight; While arcade games were the super-sellers, there was another category of home computer games far less influenced by novelty and fashion. These games continued to enjoy steady sales. Games in this category were computerized versions of old favorites such as backgammon, checkers, Mah Jong and so on. Many of these games had been around for years in computer form and some had been popular board games for centuries.

My idea was to take a traditional game from this category – one that promised lasting appeal – and combine it with an arcade game. I hoped the combination would add novelty and excitement ... and sales.

Now that may seem like an exciting enough notion to you but I doubt that you'd rush to put money on it. It's an idea, but it's a broad idea and one that needs refining before it can become a viable commercial entity.

The traditional game I selected for this great transformation was chess. Now I don't suppose that impresses you too much; there are many fine chess programs on the market and more being developed every day. But if you're yawning now, you may be a lot more interested to learn how I packaged this notion for presentation to a software house. The next section gives that presentation in its entirety.

DEATHCHESS 5000
A COMPUTER GAME
PROPOSAL

Background   Chess has long been of interest to computer programmers, largely due to the challenge it presents.

Early attempts to translate the board game into a computer game had limited results, but today there are several interesting chess programs on the market, presenting analysis of the moves to a greater or lesser depth.

New versions are still being produced, with the promotional emphasis on the "more powerful than..." approach. Chess programs play chess programs and the winner is hailed in the promotional material.

Sales of chess programs are, by definition, confined largely to chess players. It is difficult to envisage a chess program with the broad market appeal of, for example, a good arcade game.

Until now ....

DEATHCHESS 5000

Deathchess 5000 is envisioned as a game program with a market appeal far beyond that of orthodox chess. Although not necessarily structured in levels per se, it is the sort of game that can be enjoyed by any skill level, from novice to grand master.

More importantly, it can actually be played and enjoyed without any knowledge of chess whatsoever. I must admit, though, that a knowledge of chess strategy and tactics would tend to raise the game completely out of the ordinary.

Deathchess: An Overview

Deathchess 5000 would become the first computer game to combine an orthodox chess program with arcade game elements.

The combination produces an entirely new type of game, with opportunities to develop strategies very different from those of the orthodox original.

Played to its fullest potential, it would embody elements of action and excitement in addition to the purely intellectual delights of orthodox chess.

In essence, Deathchess 5000 would take us back to the roots of chess itself which, as Chatjuranga, was one of the earliest and most popular battle simulations ever devised.

The Program Described

As presently envisaged, the final program would present itself to a player in the following form:

1. Titles.

The program opens on a starscape. Tumbling towards the player, growing larger as it approaches, is a transparent, 3-D line representation of a chessboard. Animation of the board ceases when it fills the screen, with the starscape still discernible through it. At this point, animated titles would crash superimposed, held over a short delay, then faded as the program moves on to the game itself.

2. Opening game sequence.

A perfectly orthodox 64-square chessboard would appear on screen, set up with pieces to begin a game. Representation of the pieces could be the familiar Staunton shapes, but an added dimension might become the adoption of more novel "warrior" shapes to represent the pieces. There are pros and cons to both approaches. The Staunton pieces have the advantage of instant recognizability. A warrior design might prove confusing at first but would add to the overall atmosphere of the game.

3. Start of play.

Since the rules of the game are those of orthodox chess, the first move would be made by white. Again exactly like any other chess program on the market, the move would be made by keying in coded start and finish coordinates of the pawn or piece the player wishes to advance. The computer would naturally refuse to accept illegal moves, but given that the initial move is allowable, the computer (playing black) would make its own reply move. At this point, we are talking a totally straightforward chess program.

4. The action begins.

The game will continue like orthodox chess until a pawn or piece is positioned to be taken. At this point the game abruptly changes character. To illustrate this, lets examine a pawn-take-pawn move.

As the pawn-take-pawn instruction is keyed in, the chessboard fades from the screen to be replaced by an enlarged graphic of a single square set out as a battlefield. On the battlefield are two animated warrior figures – one white, one black. Each is armed with a laser rifle. The black warrior is under the control of the computer; the white under player control. The play is immediately replaced in a real-time, arcade-style action situation in which the white (pawn) warrior must, through speed and skill, kill the black warrior or be killed in his turn. The animated battle would continue until it is resolved by the death of one pawn.

5. The game continues.

Once the pawn-take-pawn warrior battle is finished, the game returns to the orthodox chessboard. The computer now stores in memory the result of the battle and accepts that as the outcome of the particular move. In other words, while white may set out to take a black pawn, white only succeeds in doing so if his warrior defeats the black warrior. If the white warrior is defeated, the game continues as if black had taken white, rather than vice versa.

6. Follow through.   The potential of this approach is limited only by computer memory and programmer imagination. Ideally, different styles of fights are envisaged – wizard battles between bishops; tank battles between rooks; mounted battles between knights (mounted on personal flyers rather than horses in this futuristic setting). Since a knight will not, of course, always battle a knight, but might have to face a pawn, bishop, rook or even queen, each piece would require fundamentally different armaments and possibly movement factors to simulate the relative strengths of the actual pieces. Nevertheless, in this version of chess, a pawn warrior might just win over an attacking knight warrior if the player was fast enough and skillful enough.

Program Considerations   The following consideration should be borne in mind in relation to the playability of the game:

1. Whatever the relative strengths, an attacking piece or pawn should be given a distinct edge over a defender. This enables much of normal chess strategy to be retained. How substantial an edge is allowed will obviously affect the overall play of the game and this is an area open to experiment during program development in order to produce the most addictive version.

2. Unlike orthodox chess, Deathchess 5000 cannot be won on a mate (which only threatens to take the opposing king in circumstances where the threat cannot be neutralized). Instead, the game is won when the opposing king is actually killed. Here again it will be important to find the optimum "battle strength" of the kings during program development.

3. Skeleton program development could almost certainly be built on an existing chess program. This need not – in fact, probably should not – be an advanced program, since the new game elements would totally overshadow any necessity for sophisticated in-depth play.

4. If possible, an option should be built in for a player vs. player game (possibly using joysticks) in addition to the basic player vs. computer version.

That, word for word, was the presentation of the idea which subsequently netted me a contract with Artic Computing Ltd., a major British software company. They followed the commonplace route of offering a lump sum for outright sale of the idea, or a percentage of royalty on the game as eventually produced. Given that the figures are agreeable, both are valid offers, although I personally would opt for the latter (and did so in this case) unless extremely short of ready cash. A royalty situation is a gamble. If the game fails to sell well, you earn little or nothing. If, on the other hand, it turns out to be a second PACMAN, then you can make a great deal of money indeed. At time of writing, I await the publication of Death-chess 5000 in the faint, but not altogether unrealistic, hope that it will make me rich.

The format of the Deathchess presentation bears closer examination, since it incorporates certain factors pertinent to the process of submitting game ideas as well as fully developed games for publication. These factors will be analyzed in the next section.

SELLING SECRETS   It could be useful for you to read through the Deathchess 5000 proposal a second time. It isn't perfect but it did sell, and it sold for reasons that have little enough to do with the central idea.

The proposal was, in fact, based upon a variety of criteria not specifically relevant to the Deathchess game that, consequently, are applicable to any idea or developed game one might wish to sell to a publisher.

The first and most important of these criteria is a clear understanding of the prospective publisher's motivation. In the book business, with which I am fairly familiar, it is still possible to find publishers whose primary interest is artistic. They are concerned with literature and, therefore, are willing to purchase books that have sufficient literary merit to justify smaller sales.

At the risk of sounding insulting, I personally have never found a game publisher who was primarily interested in anything other than the commercial success of his games. This may well be a very good thing, since I personally have never met a game designer with any other interest either. Games are games. Sometimes they are used for educational purposes but, basically, they exist to entertain and amuse, and generally have no pretensions about being works of art. In this circumstances, commerce is king.

As a game designer, your primary focus lies in getting your game published. Game publishers, however, produce new games every year and, for them, the thrill of seeing yet another colorful box in print has long since worn off. What interests the publisher, first and last, is whether or not a particular game has money-making potential. It doesn't necessarily have to be great money-making potential – publishers are realists who recognize that huge successes like MONOPOLY and TRIVIAL PURSUIT do not land on their desks every day – but it must show some commercial promise.

Recognition of this fact is the first step towards successfully selling a publisher on your game. It is pointless to tell him how wonderful the game is unless you first tell him (one way or another) how likely it is to make inroads into the market. In telling him this you must build credibility.

Dynamics of Business Relationships

The psychological dynamics of business relationships are very curious. Personal relationships may develop at their own pace, so to speak, and ripen like a piece of fruit. In business there is seldom time for this luxury. Judgments have to be made and made quickly. Such judgments are made on the basis of impressions – all too often, first impressions.

For most people in business, impressions are formed – or profoundly influenced -- by a process known as pigeonholing. You meet someone in a business context and, quite instinctively, seek a convenient mental pigeonhole in which to put him. Your contact becomes a salesperson, an accountant, executive or whatever. You realize, of course, that the label on the pigeonhole may not tell the whole story, but it is a starting point and one that allows you to deal with the other person conveniently.

The problem with all this is that while you are neatly pigeonholing those you meet in business, they are quietly engaged in exactly the same process with you. Most companies play this game instinctively and show great concern not only for the collective corporate image, but also for the image presented by individual personnel. This is why salesmen often dress as conservatively as the chairman of the board, while the artists employed by advertising agencies invariably often look like Toulouse-Lautrec with lifts in his shoes. In the first instance, the salesmen are striving for respectability. In the second, the artists are attempting to be pigeonholed as "creative".

How you are pigeonholed depends, almost entirely, on the image you present. This is something worth thinking about before approaching a potential game publisher. A creative image is dramatic and attention-getting, but I personally have found it far more useful to project a hard-nosed image of marketing expertise. Publishers, who are marketing people themselves, feel at home with other marketing people. Once you are pigeonholed as a marketing expert, you cease to be looked upon as just another creative weirdo with a bizarre game idea, and become the producer of a product that has commercial potential. A marketeer's image is no guarantee that a publisher will buy your game, but if the image is successfully projected, it will virtually guarantee that your proposal will at least be carefully considered.

If you reread the Deathchess proposal in light of these comments, you will quickly discover it is written from a marketeer's viewpoint. The opening section, entitled "Background", has already used the word "market" by the second paragraph and talks about market appeal by the fourth. Even before you get into the description of the game proper, its potential appeal is being hyped ("far beyond that of orthodox chess") and you are psychologically set up to make a positive buying decision.

The proposal's short overview emphasizes that a new type of game is being offered. After all, novelty has a market appeal all its own. The overview further specifies that this game falls into both the long-selling chess and fast-selling arcade game categories. (It might be worth mentioning at this point that the Deathchess proposal was offered at a time when arcade games were still super-sellers in the British market, despite the fact that they had taken somewhat of a tumble in the U.S.)

The Proposal Should be Businesslike and Professional

The format of the proposal is businesslike and methodical, reinforcing a professional image. The style is enthusiastic, but not overly so, for many good ideas have been lost due to overkill. The object was to write a proposal as a fellow businessman. Such an approach usually commands more respect than an emotional hard-sell from a "creative" designer. When viewed in this light, the game itself becomes secondary.

The question of image goes far beyond whether you project yourself as a marketeer. Such a projection happens to be one of my favorites (possibly because I am a marketeer in many aspects of my career) but I'm aware it's not the only effective image. A track record as a successful game designer would be just as good, if not better. So would kudos in some other industry or profession. No matter the image you wish to present, your proposal must be professional. Satisfying this criterion is essential, whether marketing a fully developed game or just a bare idea.

DON'T FORGET THE PLAYTEST

Creating a game is only a tenth of the battle when you want to sell to a publisher. Your next step is the playtest; and it's a step you have to take before you even start to think about the submission process.

Games may be a lot of fun in theory, but may crash completely when actually played. I recall investing a small fortune several years ago in an imported European game as a Christmas present for my stepson. You will not be unduly amazed to learn I buy games the way other fathers buy train sets - and substantially for the same reason - because I get to play the games as well.

This particular offering grabbed me at once. The box art was superb. The game was a science fiction board game and when the storekeeper let me take a peek inside, I saw that the box was full of gorgeous colorful pieces and cards. The whole package had a quality air and smelled like a real winner.

It wasn't. To this day the game has never been played in my house, either by its proud new owner or anyone else. This might have been due to poor translation - the game originated in Spain - but I doubt it. The rules were clear enough: putting them into practice was another matter. My guess is that despite the enormous talent (not to mention money) that went into the finished packaging, somebody forgot about playtesting.

A Critically Important Step

Playtesting lets you know where you've gone wrong in a game, where the weaknesses lie and, above all, where it lacks clarity. Clarity is critically important. When you develop a game, many of its aspects may be obvious to you, but not to someone who hasn't sweated blood on the project for months. A good playtester will let you know that the game tripped him up. A good designer will take out all the obstacles before submission. It's well to remember that if a publisher is interested, the very first thing he's going to do is playtest, so the effort invested before submission will be worthwhile.

Once you have found a publisher who has agreed to examine your game (never – under any circumstances – send one until the publisher has agreed), make sure it goes out ready to play. Don't ever send in a prototype with a note instructing the prospective party to find his own game money or to just use checkers for the men. Game publishers want something they can pass directly on to their playtesters and they don't look at the product again until the initial playtest reports come back.

Sending a Prototype to a Publisher

It's also a good idea to send the prototype in a box rather than an envelope, making certain all the playing pieces are separated and secured to keep them from getting jumbled in the mail. A beneficial rule of thumb is: the better a first impression the prototype makes, the better its chances are of being given serious consideration all the way up the line – from playtesting to marketing.

Several years ago something happened to me that proves that last point. I received a unique inquiry from a designer wanting to submit a game. Rather than send a letter, the enterprising fellow sent a short one-act play purportedly set in my office, consisting of dialogue between the designer and myself. The approach was so clever I felt I had to give the fellow a chance, and I wrote back saying we'd examine the game – but, no promises.

My jaw hit the floor when the prototype arrived on my desk. It was nothing short of beautiful. At first I thought it had already been printed but close examination revealed it to be a cunning and professional job by an expert graphic artist. The game really scored big points by making me aware the inventor cared enough to spend the money to show it in such an excellent light.

After examining all the gorgeous components, I looked at the rules. Seeing that they were well-written and noting that the subject matter held marketing possibilities, I sent it on to the playtesters.

When the report came back my jaw dropped again. The playtesters had accomplished something very rare for a game company: they found the game to have virtually no play value whatsoever. Dumbfounded, I sent it out again, to a different set of playtesters. The report came back the same. The point is, the prototype was so well made and so enticing that I was fooled into wasting my time and that of two groups of playtesters on a game that otherwise would have been sent back the same day it arrived.

A WORD ABOUT GAME AGENTS

About once a week an enthusiastic game inventor will call on me to ask if I can recommend a game agent to present his or her game to prospective publishers. Like literary agents, game agents sell their clients' works for a share of the royalties. Both types of agents are practically inaccessible to first time inventors or authors, but they differ in that legitimate game agents are about as hard to find as publishing contracts.

Of all the people I've known in the game industry there are only two who specialize as agents and they don't want their names mentioned in this book for a number of reasons. First, they both have other careers and work only part time as agents and, second, they'd hang me if their phones started ringing off the hook with calls from novice game inventors.

There are those, however, who prey on starry-eyed beginners. They have companies that will take your game, conduct a three-day market study, generate a fill-in-the-blank computer presentation and "sell" your idea to a game manufacturer. They'll do all this for you for a very modest up-front fee of perhaps $500 or more plus a percentage, in the unlikely event that they get lucky and some publisher really does read and/or buy their stale proposal.

Check Them Out Carefully

I do not mean to say uncategorically that all such marketing and market research firms are worthless. Legitimate ones are invaluable, but I have never met anyone who sold their game or game idea to a publisher by paying this type of firm to represent them. If you're considering taking this path just be sure to be careful. Check out the firm first. Ask to see a list of games they've sold in the past. Then ask for a client list you can call on, to learn first hand what kind of firm they are before you hand over your hard earned money.

It might be possible to find a legitimate agent or two by checking with trade associations (the Toy Manufacturers Association, for example) or by calling the association's member game producers for a recommendation. If an agent agrees to first look at a design from a new inventor, then attempts to sell it and is successful, the inventor can expect to pay about half of all future royalties. On the positive side, legitimate agents rarely ask for money in advance except to cover specific expenses.

LAST WORDS ON SELLING YOUR GAME

If your goal is to sell your game to an existing publisher, you've picked a tough, but not impossible, nut to crack. Persistence and a professional, creative approach are the necessary tools. You may have to use several approaches several times with a number of different publishers so don't allow yourself to become discouraged or gun-shy about contacting potential game houses. If you are creatively persistent, and you are trying to promote a product that has market potential, keep pitching. If the fast ball doesn't get the job done, try the slider or change-up.

How tough is it really? There are two rumors floating around about how a couple of ingenious game inventors managed to get big firms to look at, and eventually accept, their games. The first chap, so the story goes, had tried everything. Determined not to waste any more postage he took vacation time off work and drove to a targeted game company's headquarters. He made a picket sign saying "Take Pity, Look At My Game!", draped it over his shoulders and greeted the company's employees and executives as they drove in to work in the mornings. The second fellow allegedly "borrowed" a well-known name from the game industry and illegally used it as an endorsement for his product. If the story is correct, he got his game published, but if he loses the resulting lawsuit he'll be destitute.

An Off-the-Wall Approach

One final ploy a friend told me about will work as well for you as for the guy who dreamed it up. A man involved in selling investment plans through direct mail advertising would type a letter and send it to a prospective client. If he didn't get a response within three weeks, he'd type an exact duplicate of the letter, then wad it up as if it had been placed in the trash. Next, he'd smooth it out and, using a bold marker, write across the top, "Please do not throw this away again"; then he sent it back to the name on the mailing list. It's crazy, but it got attention in a creative way. If you're to have any success at all in getting a major company to examine your game, you must be creative.

There are a lot of people out there with game ideas, nearly as many as there are with great unwritten novels. The competition is stiff and the odds are heavily against success. If you do become that one in a million and your game makes you wealthy, all I can say is congratulations, more power to you, you deserve everything you get. Now if I could just get some book publisher to look at this "Great American Novel" I'm writing ...

SELF-PUBLISHING

Now that my friend Herbie and I have taken you down the Yellow Brick Road to show you how to submit work to publishers, it's time to get back into my Wicked-Witch-of-the-East costume. I am assuming, incorrectly I hope, that you've been unable to sell your game to a publisher but are still determined to see it settled in the marketplace – which means doing it yourself. Here goes then. The first step is to answer this question ...

SHOULD I REALLY DO IT?

To decide whether a game is worth making, first do some homework. Determine if it is similar to others already on the market. People in the gaming industry are deluged with new games every day, but few are truly unique. Search hard enough and you'll find games similar to your own although, hopefully, none will be too similar. Once you've been able to ascertain this, find out how well the games did. Usually this can be accomplished by buddying up to merchants who have sold games for a number of years. Locate one with a good memory and he or she can prove to be a gold mine of information. In most cases retailers only remember two types of games – those that sold extremely well and those that didn't sell at all.

You may find games similar to your own still being sold. The simplest way to check this is to go into stores that have a decent supply of board games and spend some time there examining the stock, making sure to read the backs of the boxes. Once you've identified several games as being similar to your design, try to obtain copies. Find out who made them. Check the copyright date, then look for the latest edition or printing. Find out how well they did, or are doing. Try to find advertisements for the game. Ask friends, family and neighbors if they've ever heard of it or played it. Remember, if it's similar, this will say a good bit about how your game is going to be received.

Once you've studied some of these other games, get people – not family – to play them. Captive audiences simply won't net any real insight. If the game is similar in subject matter, you'll be surprised how much information can be picked up just by paying attention to the attitudes of those asked to participate. While playing just relax and enjoy the game, making it enjoyable for others. Don't make constant comparisons to your own game. After play is finished, analyze the game relative to your own. Determine the ways in which your game is better and what can be done to improve on it.

DEFINE YOUR MARKET

The next step is to study the market, and this requires more research. Start by defining the theme or subject matter of your game. For instance: MONOPOLY has real-estate as its theme, RISK offers an abstract world war background, SCRABBLE is a crossword puzzle game. Once the underlying theme has been identified, determine what and where its markets are going to be. Subjects with limited market appeal – such as the book by the dog-breeding lady – offer the advantage of attracting small groups of people likely to be interested in the product at a reasonable cost. Mass market appeal items have a much wider population spread on which to base sales but it is much more expensive to reach their diverse audience.

Once you've tagged your game with a theme and have been able to identify its market, put it under a mathematical microscope to determine its sales potential and the best marketing approach. How many people are there in the specific market? What percentage of them would be interested in buying the game? Are they mostly men, women, children, or a combination? What age group is involved and what is the average income? Where do these people shop? What magazines do they read? What television shows do they watch?

A Hypothetical Case History

To hypothesize, let's say we are researching a game based on the American Civil War. This is a limited market, thus making it easier to define but harder to generate mass sales, relative to a more general market. A quick trip to the local library yields a dozen magazines devoted exclusively to this theme. A few letters or phone calls and a couple of weeks later we get some advertising information from these magazines. We discover the largest, in terms of circulation, is the *Civil War Times Illustrated*. We find it has over 100,000 readers, a large enough base to make analysis meaningful. After all, the circulation of all the civil war magazines, allowing for duplication, is around 300,000.

The demographics of the magazines indicate the average reader is male, age 33 with an annual income of $22,000. So far so good, right? Maybe! A thirty-three-year-old man doesn't sound like a person who plays many games. But, suppose our man is married, has 1.7 children and spends a great deal of time reading, writing and participating in other indoor activities. If we're lucky the demographics might even reveal how many of these men play board games, for some magazines do ask this question on their survey forms.

Advertising Demographics Are Important

Now we know the right profile to which our ads should be geared. Thumbing through back issues of the magazine, and keeping notes on the kinds of ads that appear, especially in issue after issue, we can determine what appeals best to the readers. If an ad for another game about the Civil War is spotted don't panic. I said very few games were truly unique. Instead, write down the name and address of the company. After cataloging the advertisements in the magazines, contact the company, and order the game or look for it in stores. If no store within a 100-mile radius has heard of it, there's a chance it is being produced by someone just like you, which may be a break. People who publish their own games like to talk about them. Give the company a call after seeing (preferably playing) the game and finding something nice to say about it. Ask questions about the play and design. When the designer starts talking, tell him where you saw the ad and inquire about other ad placements. It's amazing how much information people will share.

So, we found the ad, ordered the game and called the person who produced it. He tells us, "Yeah, my CWT ad pulls ok, but the wargamers are really eating it up".

"What", we ask, "are wargamers?"

Wargamers: A Large Group

He explains that wargamers are a group of people who play – predictably – games about wars. Prodding him, we finally get the names of six 'wargame' magazines. A quick trip back to the library's guide to periodicals shows us that another market has just been discovered.

Repeating the procedure of contacting magazine publishers we receive more information. We estimate that this other market contains another 200,000 devotees, giving us a total of 500,000 potential customers who are already interested in the subject of our game.

Now we're getting somewhere: half a million people who are interested in the American Civil War to some extent, and 200,000 of them are known gamers. Yes, indeed, it looks like we've struck pay-dirt! Let's apply some rules of thumb and see where we really are.

Nearly every marketing or advertising book presents a set of formulas which will supposedly tell how to determine advertising response. None of them guarantee anything, of course, but they all claim to be fairly accurate. Not to be outdone, here is my own formula for results obtained from placing ads in specialized magazines. I've found it to be reasonably accurate – at least as accurate as the textbook approaches.

Approximately 10% of the readers of a magazine will read a full page ad. (If the ad is in color the percentage will go up; if the ad is not full page the percentage will go down). Of the 10% who spend 30 to 60 seconds reading the ad, perhaps 1% will order the item – assuming it is competitively priced and looks like quality merchandise. Now, where does that put us?

Figuring Advertising Response

Ten percent of 500,000 is 50,000. One percent of 50,000 is 500. So – using my rule of thumb — if you have a good ad, a good product, and a decent price, you could expect to sell 500 copies of the Civil War game by placing a full page ad in each of the magazines you've discovered. If most of these are mail order sales at full retail price, you should do okay. It used to be that only one out of every ten Americans ordered anything by direct mail, but that percentage has been increasing in recent years, stimulated by fuel price increases and the rising number of two-income households where both partners work all day.

Finished? Not yet! Flip through the war game magazines looking at the kind of ads that keep recurring. Suddenly you spot yet another ad for another Civil War game, but this time in the classified section. Wondering why in the world wargamers would advertise here, you scan the page and see an interesting little ad in the corner. It's about Civil War Reenactment groups (people who dress up like Civil War soldiers from a particular regiment and go on camping trips). Now you've hit upon another potential market. Starting to get the idea?

Read those magazines! Study them from cover to cover, inside and out. They not only can identify new markets that might otherwise take you years to find, they also can lead to other magazines in those markets.

If you feel your game is not a special interest item and you don't need to go through all this, you're missing a bet. Besides, unless you have enough money to remake *The Ten Commandments*, you don't have enough money to advertise on television or in such general interest magazines *Time*, *People*, *Playboy* or even *Games*. In short, you have to start getting the game on the market someplace and you've got to create enough beginning sales to at least generate word-of-mouth advertising for the product.

General Interest Games

Let's take another approach, with a game more general in nature. This time we've got a game similar to SCRABBLE or BOGGLE. It's a word game, about as general as they come. Our task is to find places to advertise that, while relatively inexpensive, still will reach a potentially high interest market. The first and most obvious places to investigate are the 'crossword' and word puzzle magazines. Then, think about who else would be interested in words. There's MENSA, an organization whose members have extremely high IQs. Say, don't they have a mailing list of all their members, and I think someone once told me they run a wholesale operation and have a monthly newsletter. What about writers and would-be writers? They have an intense interest in words and there are several writers' magazines. I'll bet a special ad could be slanted for that market. And then there's...

The point is, no matter what the game's theme you should be able to identify, locate, and analyze potential markets. All it takes is a little imagination and intelligence – and a lot of research. If you don't seem to be making headway at first, or if you begin to get bored, just remember: this information is vital. Without it as a starting reference you're lost before you have even begun.

CALLING ALL VENDORS

By now you have designed a game or you at least have one in mind. You have found and categorized a number of markets and estimated the amount of advertising space you will need and calculated the costs involved. You probably have played the game so often that the family hides on Saturday nights. You're ready ... so, what's next?

It's time to make some preliminary phone calls to local printers, box and board makers. You'll find that a host of them are listed in the yellow pages. Be straightforward with them: they aren't sitting there waiting to steal your idea. Ask them the exact dimensions of the largest game board they can make or have made locally and the same for the game box. There's no sense in designing a game that can't be produced, but you should bear in mind that the bigger the item, the more it will cost. Be sure to ask the printers the size of the largest 'image area' they can print. This is slightly smaller than the largest sheet they can run through their presses and represents the area where the ink is placed. A good standard is 25' by 38'. Most printers can handle this size, so make sure to design the components to a standard that will allow competitive bids. Once the sheet sizes are established, design everything to fit on as few sheets as possible. For example, if a game requires a deck of cards, change the size of the cards to get the deck on one press run. In printing the cardinal rule is: the fewer the press sheets, the less expensive the job.

Working With Printers

If you are fortunate enough to live in an area near a printer with experience in producing games, you probably will discover two things:

1. You'll get a fair price and,

2. He will save you time, mistakes, and money by handling production entirely.

You will pay a bit of a premium for this total capability, but it's worth it; better than your coordinating all the steps involved – from product assembly to storage. If you find someone like this, check him out first to be sure he does in fact produce games on a regular basis. If so, be grateful for your luck.

Armed with this information, make a prototype, redoing the original if it is too large. List every item in the game, (even the most obvious), beginning with the box. Failure to communicate to the artist all the elements involved – even those that are obvious to you – could cost you a lot of extra money; additional expenses that could be avoided. Make sure you know all the "facts" in precise detail; for example, the quantity of each denomination of play money in your game, the size of the money, the number and size of any game cards, the number of tokens, the number of colors to print on the board and whether the money will be printed on both sides or only one. Decide on the box top design – is it going to be a color photograph, an illustration or a multi-colored design and, if the latter, in how many colors. Itemize every aspect of every component before taking it to show anyone.

Graphic artists and printers are busy people. If you show up and say, "Well, look guys, I've got this game I want you to make. It's about so big, and the box has got to be real pretty, and it's just, gee whiz, a heck of a lot of fun to play," they are going to show you the door politely and give you the name of a competitor whom they would dearly love to see take on this job.

Finding A Graphic Artist

When you meet the person who is going to do your final artwork, have a finished prototype ready in the right size, and all the components done to the best of your ability. The artist will need these for reference. For initial discussions have several copies of your itemized list of components showing sizes, numbers and colors.

At this point you should become a bit of a horse trader. If you're smart, you'll find a commercial artist who doesn't have a fancy office (he might even work out of his home) or a large ad in the yellow pages. You're not a big-time game company yet and there's no point in paying for extra overhead. Sit down with the artist and go over the entire list. Don't skip anything. Most artists tend to miss details until it comes time for them to make up their invoices. After every item has been discussed, including the method of doing four-color art for the board and box top, ask the artist to provide a quote for the entire job. If he refuses or says he'd rather charge by the hour, make excuses and find another designer – you have come to the wrong place.

It will take several such interviews to obtain and determine the best price. Notice I didn't say the lowest price. Make sure, when comparing the estimates, that you're comparing apples with apples. Don't be misled just because one price is substantially lower than the others. On the contrary, be suspicious of very low bids. After settling on two or three fair quotes, go back to the artists and point out to them that this is a highly speculative venture. Make it clear that you don't have tons of money and suggest a trade-off: a price reduction in exchange for, say, six months to finish the artwork, so that it can be completed during slow times. Sometimes this works, sometimes it doesn't; but it's worth a shot, assuming you can wait six months.

A final but often overlooked criterion in selecting an artist is the necessity of finding someone with whom you are comfortable. You are going to be spending a lot of time together and, most likely, at some point you're going to have to be critical about some error in production. You want to be able to make your point without incurring the artist's wrath. Hell hath no fury ...

Box Design Is Very Important

When getting down to basics, don't skimp on the box top, side panels, and back. These are the most important pieces of art in a game. The illustration and overall design of the box top and sides have to be strong; eye-catching enough to make people notice it and pick it out from all the other games surrounding it on the shelves. Once the potential consumer has the game in hand, the "hype" on the back of the box absolutely has to be able to convince people they have no choice but to buy it. It not only has to make them want it, it should make them feel they just can't live without it. You and the artist, but especially you, should put a lot of thought into these areas. You should already have looked at hundreds of game boxes and decided on the basic approach before meeting with a potential artist. Basic approach, however, means flexibility. I've found it best, when dealing with sensitive artists (and I haven't found one yet who wasn't sensitive) to tell them what you envision – colors, ideas, concepts, images — then let them go to work. Don't give them complete freedom, but just enough to allow them to think of the work as their own creation. Artists are most happy when they are putting their creative talents to work with as little supervision as possible

Working With An Artist — A True Story

All of this reminds me of my first experience with an artist. I was living outside Atlanta, Georgia and was working on my very first game. I had gone in to see a printer – one of the biggest in Atlanta. His office was in an impressive five-story building near the downtown area. I was taken into a posh conference room and waited for my assigned agent. (They didn't call them salesmen in this place.) He came in wearing a very expensive suit, a stylish haircut, and manicured nails. Offering me a drink, he pulled out a hidden bar from inside one of the walls. When he sat down I began to talk. "I've got this game," I said. "It's about this big and gee whiz, is it ever a lot of fun to play". He listened to me for a few minutes, nodding his head and looking at his watch. When I finished he told me he'd be right back, left the room and returned with a sheet of paper on which he had written the names and phone numbers of an artist and a smaller print company which, he assured me, would suit me better. Because he was generous enough to tell me I should see the artist before the print company I was spared making a complete fool of myself a second time.

I called the artist that afternoon – interrupting his nap, I suspected – and asked to see him. He told me to hold on and, in muffled tones, said to his receptionist, who was also his wife, "There's another looney-tune on the phone. Can you get the place cleaned up by tomorrow?" I didn't hear her answer but it must have been affirmative because he came back on the line, saying the only time he could spare would be during his lunch hour the next day.

We made an appointment and I showed up, eager to get my game in the works. When I arrived at the one-room office, which was partitioned into a receptionist/secretary area and a two-drawing-board work area, I was shown past the partition to a man a little older than myself. He was frantically cutting and pasting columns of galleys to art boards. (I learned later, after we'd become friends, that it was all faked, designed to impress would-be clients.) He asked to see my game and, because of the fiasco I'd had the day before, I also gave him what I considered to be a complete list of components. I laid everything out before him, afraid to speak in case I made a fool of myself again. He looked it all over, shaking his head from side to side, letting out a solemn 'Hmmm' every now and then. When he finished he looked at me and asked, "Are you sure you want to do this?" I nodded, grinning stupidly. His next question was, "Who do you think will buy it?"

I proceeded to explain my marketing strategy, such as it was, and made an effort to convince him that I not only was serious about doing the game but that I also knew more than he might realize. I must not have been too convincing because the next words out of his mouth were, "Do you have any money?"

Now we were in an area I could handle. "A little," I replied. "How much is all this going to cost?" Understand, way back then, which is longer ago than I care to admit, things were a lot cheaper. "A thousand dollars," responded the man at the drawing board, turning away to hide an irrepressible grin.

"Gee, I don't have anywhere near that," I admitted, pausing for a reaction. Getting none, I stammered, "Gosh, I'm sorry I bothered you. I had no idea it would cost so much. I'm really embarrassed and sorry I wasted so much time." I got up and started gathering my material. This is where the dialogue really began to roll.

HE: "How much do you have?" (He wasn't about to let this fish off the hook.)

ME: "Well, let's see. After printing and die cutting and, oh yeah, making the boxes, I've only got about ... oh, forget it. I'm ashamed to tell you." (I continued to bundle up my items, but slowly.)

HE: "I might be able to do it for less if you give me time to work it in between jobs, but you'll have to leave me alone. Don't be calling me every other day, bugging me. How much do you have?" (He was showing more submissiveness than I dared hope.)

ME: (with my most sheepish look):"Well, gee, this is embarrassing, I've only got about $250."

He looked astonished, hurt, insulted. I shrugged my shoulders and turned to leave. "I'll do it for $500 but you've got to give me four months; no ifs, ands or buts," he said, glaring at me through his thick glasses.

That moment, as Bogart once said, was the beginning of a beautiful friendship. This guy turned out to be a hell of an artist. He was fast, dependable and reasonably priced. He helped produce my first thirteen games and contributed mightily to their success. For those who are interested, he's still in the Atlanta area working out of his home and providing professional skills and services to his clients.

Of course, there were drawbacks. He would work all night to meet a deadline but wanted to be sure that I was working all night myself. He could be crabby and cantankerous, or gentle and generous; you just never knew until you spoke to him. He had the temperament of an artist - moody and unpredictable – but with that a strong sense of responsibility. We became great friends throughout the years and, to this day, he is one of the few things I miss about Atlanta.

Enough old memories! Now back to business!

THE PRINTING PROCESS

The artist you select is going to be your guide and translator in the world of printing. He is going to teach you in depth what I am providing only in passing – an understanding of the terminology you'll be hearing. This may seem unnecessary, but misunderstanding what people are talking about will cost you money. There is a glossary of printing and art terms included at the back of this book. Take some time to become familiar with them.

Right now we'll be sticking to art talk, though some of it will overlap into printing. As I have said already, the most important piece of art in your game is the box top, sometimes known as the wrap or label. Its job is to get prospective buyers to select your game from among all the others.

There are basically three art mediums for box wraps: a full- color illustration or photograph using the process known as four-color separation; a graphic design of one or more colors accomplished by mechanical separation; and a combination of the two.

Since this is going to be an expensive and important piece of art, spend some time planning and considering the alternatives. More than likely, you'll wind up using the four-color separation process. It's not cheap but it can be far less expensive than mechanical art which requires a lot of stripping.

Stripping... Not What You Think

Stripping is an art involving the skill of craftsmen. A good stripper has the eye of an eagle. He can cut, position and fasten pieces of film shaped in long strips in such a fashion as to create the most intricate and beautiful patterns of colors imaginable. Using only the three primary colors (blue, red, yellow) and black (hence the term, 'four-color process' or 'printing'), a stripper can work the negatives to create an endless rainbow of colors, shades and hues. The problem is good strippers are not only hard to find, but they don't work cheap. Of course, in today's world where the march of technology never ceases, computerized machines are being developed to replace not only strippers, but eventually most aspects of the graphic arts. Currently, the machines are too costly to pose an immediate threat but by the turn of the century the stripping and separations required for printing jobs will vary, based on the number of special effects rather than the number of colors. For the time being, if your artist tries to talk you into doing an all mechanical, multi-colored piece of art, make sure he plans on separating the colors mechanically on different overlays.

Back to basics again. The kind of printing involved here is known as 'off-set'. It's called this because a roller picks up ink from the 'well' and transfers it to another roller containing a metal plate bearing the image of what is being printed. This plate, now wet with ink, meets yet another rubber roller and transfers an impression to it. That roller meets a final roller carrying a sheet of paper and imprints the image upon it. The concept, supposedly, was first invented by an Egyptian somewhere around 2,000 B.C., who made a crude, manual off-set press from smooth stones, bees' wax, oil and ink. In any event, using this type of printing and four-color process, any picture and virtually any number of colors may be printed. If the printer has a four-color press, one which puts down all four colors as the paper travels through it, the paper is blank when it goes in and finished when it comes out.

Most people take printing, especially quality printing, for granted. They may remark, "Gee, that's nice," when they see a particularly attractive printed piece, without understanding they are seeing an intricate and complex pattern composed of individual dots invisible to the naked eye. These tiny dots, called screens, are the secret of four-color printing. By combining these screens any color can be made from the primary colors and black.

ART FOR THE BOX TOP

It's important to understand the difference between four-color process separation and mechanical separation. The latter may be done for four-color printing, by hand-stripping and using combinations of dot screens at varying angles with individual camera shots. If the art is simple enough, this method will be cheaper than having a full color separation made. A four-color process separation is done with a camera or, in some high-tech operations, with devices employing lasers and computers. If your art is an illustration, photograph or complex, multi-colored design, this will probably be the least expensive way to go. Most likely, the art will be a combination of illustration and type, especially for the game's title.

Now that some of what the artist does makes sense to you let's discuss the type of art to be used for the wrap. Incidentally, it is a rare artist indeed whose verbal communication skills come close to matching his artistic talents.

Whether the artist wants to do an illustration, a painting or a full color drawing, make sure you're comfortable with his style as well as being able to live with his price. Don't be afraid of hurting his feelings on either account. If he goes through with it and winds up doing something awful, you'll still be obligated to pay. You can gauge whether he or she has the ability to get the results you want partly by looking through a portfolio (all artists have these, to show their past works to prospective clients). If you aren't able to settle on an illustration or a price, or if you just don't think the artist can deliver the quality you want, it may be time to head back to the library to look for existing photographs or paintings.

Cutting Costs in the Box Top Design

Nearly every library has a collection of magazines. Pore through the ones specifically for photographers, looking for a photo that seems ideal or close to it, for your cover. If you can find one it will probably save you a good bit of money, because the photographer of the picture generally will permit it to be used, for a modest sum, so long as he receives credit (name and address) in the rules of your game. If you can't come up with anything after going through all the magazines, don't give up. Switch to art prints and art books.

Over the years thousands, perhaps millions, of scenes have been painted and preserved in print. Look long enough and you'll find a famous, or near famous, piece of art that will work very nicely. This research could be a bonanza for you, for several reasons. If you come up with a picture that is very old, it probably is in the public domain, which means that it can be used legally without paying anyone for the right to do so. Thus, you could find an illustration for your game without having to pay an artist $800 or more to create it.

While looking through the magazines and prints, don't be narrow-minded. Be open to box wraps the images may suggest. Who knows, one of them might offer a better idea than what you had in mind.

Once you have an illustration for the cover and show it to the artist, he will probably find all manner of things wrong with it, since he didn't do it or get paid for it. Don't let that bother you – it comes with the territory. What's needed now is to select a typestyle for the title and subtitle of the game – something befitting both the illustration and the game theme. The artist should have pretty much free rein here. With his knowledge of type faces he can select half a dozen or so from which you can choose. The only other alternative is for you to spend a day or two yourself going through page after page of type books, looking at thousands of type styles.

The next step is to select a background color to border the illustration and wrap around the sides of the box. It should complement the illustration, yet be bright and solid to give life to the side panels. After making your choice, decide on a color for the type faces that will appear on both the top and the sides. This color should contrast with the background. When you've reached a decision, leave the artist alone until he's finished. If he needs you, he'll call.

Sharing this with you reminds me of two experiences I had with box wraps. I was working with the artist I mentioned earlier and the first episode was with the fifth or sixth game I'd done. Mike, the artist, always said, "You know enough about printing to be dangerous," and I'm afraid this story proves his point. The game was called SUB-MARINE. I'd found this marvelous photograph of a submarine surfacing at night, illuminated by an exploding freighter. It was perfect except for one thing: it was in black and white. By then I knew enough to know the box wrap needed color and, being of Scottish ancestry, I could not resist attempting a two color mechanical cover to save money.

I suggested to Mike, as I showed him a rough sketch alongside the photograph, he enlarge the photograph to the proper size, cut a mechanical separation on an overlay for the bright area of the explosion and make the type white. The effect would be an all black box with bold white type and a bright yellow area in the center for contrast and color. (White does not count as a color if the paper is white and is reversed out of an ink.)

Mike felt this wouldn't work, saying he should 'airbrush' (a painting technique) the yellow area and have it separated. Being cheap, and thinking I knew more than I did, I told him no. I was sure it would work fine.

Needless to say, it didn't. When the job came off the press parts of the yellow area had blended with the black ink to create a hideous green tinge to the whole affair. It was horrible. But in those days, as is the case today, I didn't have all the money in the world and I had to live with it. Fortunately for me, it was a limited print run that sold fairly quickly. Then I managed to sell the game to another company before I had to worry about reprinting.

The second episode had a somewhat more pleasing outcome. I think it was my tenth game, one with a science fiction theme. By chance I had seen a color photograph of the Crab Nebula taken by an observatory. It was beautiful, containing subtle shifts of reds, blues, greens and yellows against a midnight blue, star-filled background. I wrote to the observatory, asking the cost of the negative, with the intention of using the photograph on the box top. Two weeks later I received a four-by-five inch color transparency and a bill for $16. The artist dropped the type into the area occupied by the photo and the box wrap was done. It was simple, gorgeous, and eye-catching.

Listen to the Experts!   The point of the first story: Always listen to artists and printers, no matter how much you think you know. Printing is one of those professions plagued with details. In all the years I have been associated with it, I've never met anyone who knew everything about every aspect of it.

The point of the second story: Sometimes simple is best. Not every box wrap has to be a complicated masterpiece. As long as it fulfills the main objectives of being attractive, attention-getting, and effective in its statement about the game's theme, it could be something as ordinary as a black box. But don't use that. Someone else has already done it.

GAMEBOARD ART

When the box top is finished, the next item to tackle is the gameboard. Most gameboards are large enough physically and simple enough graphically to be set up for mechanical separations. When four-color process separations are done the charge is basically by the square inch, and a twenty-by-twenty gameboard is an awful lot of square inches.

When planning the art for the game board make sure to adhere to the theme, keeping colors complementary to each other as well as to the box wrap and using the same or compatible type styles. In other words, try to remain consistent throughout the art work. Many first-time game producers are advised to keep their package colorful, so they try to make each component a different and brighter color than the one before. Pretty soon the whole thing winds up looking like a Mexican circus. Color is important, but so is pleasing the eye. Stay consistent and the game will look like a well-conceived, quality product. Bounce around with colors and your product will send a message that it is for juveniles only – not a market limitation you want to impose on your own brainchild.

Watch Your Tolerances

A few final comments on box and board artwork; pay strict attention to your finishing touches. For instance, Be sure to leave enough tolerance on the box and board artwork. Tolerance is the distance from the edges of the finished art to the edge of the actual box top or game board. Usually one-eighth of an inch is enough. Also – please forgive me if this advice seems unnecessary – take care that the gameboard, when folded, will fit in your box. This is a silly mistake, but I've seen more than one person go crying to their artist when box and boards were delivered and did not fit.

If you're dead-set on having an illustration executed by an artist, but aren't satisfied with the particular artist you have engaged for graphics, find another one for the illustrations. It's not uncommon for good graphic artists to be terrible illustrators, or vice versa. Don't be embarrassed to tell a graphic artist that an illustrator is doing your box wrap art.

THE FINAL WRAP

There are a couple of reasons why the box top and game board were finished first. One is that they make a statement about the theme of the game and set a standard or guide for the art that is to follow. Another reason is that they take the longest to reach completion as they not only have to be printed but also must be fabricated into boxes and boards. The last essential item to work on is the box bottom, since half a box won't do any good at all.

The most important thing about box bottom art is what it says and how it says it. Its sole reason for existing is to make people buy the game. A good way to get a handle on this aspect of selling is to go back to the stores and read every box back with a front that grabs your attention. Check to see how many games are displayed so that only one side panel is visible and you'll understand the importance of including a line or two of selling copy on these surfaces. Take great care in writing the copy for the box back. If the box top is really good and does its job of getting people to pick the game up, you still are only halfway there. The critical half is actually convincing people to buy the game; it would be a shame if the box back did not fulfill its part of this obligation.

Once the box top art is finished, have the artist determine the image area for the press on which it is to run. If it's not too large and is being printed in process colors, it won't cost too much to have a box back printed at the same time, on the same sheet of paper. If this can be done, you'll not only save money for a one-color (black type) box back, but for a little extra you can also add some color to the back of the box as well. Remember, color – anywhere on the box – does help sell. If the box wrap art image area is too large to allow the back to run at the same time, it's best to stick with a one-color box back printed on a cheaper grade of paper. It won't look as nice, but the main thing about the back is what it says. Sure, good looks help, but when there's a limited budget, this is a good place to save.

While you're trying out box back copy on friends and co-workers, the artist can do the layout and paste-up for the game's other components. This is assuming, of course, that the game has been thoroughly play-tested, the component mix is correct and the rules are so clear even a Supreme Court Justice couldn't misinterpret them. In order to save money and possible embarrassment later on, there are a few things the artist should have worked out in advance. In case he didn't, I'll go over them.

Cards, Game Money, etc.

It's likely your game will make use of one or more decks of cards, game money, play stock certificates, etc. These items can become exorbitantly expensive if not handled properly, so try to avoid being charged for any more hand labor than is absolutely necessary. For instance, if you don't employ a printer with a card collating machine, your customers are not going to find neatly sorted stacks of game money or cards separated into nice little trays when they open the game package. Instead, they'll have a clean-looking sheet of money that has been carefully perforated, for them to tear and sort; or a large folded sheet of cards die-cut and nicked on the edges to hold them in place until the customer punches them out and gathers them into decks. At least five years ago this would have been the case for most game makers. Now there are many companies capable of automatically cutting and collating decks of cards or stacks of money, and it's just about as economical as the alternative mentioned above. It's possible, because of location and shipping costs, that you will have to go the non-automated route.

"What happened to quality?" you scream. "Is it being thrown out the window?"

Hardly. Many major game companies have adopted this technique. If you have been doing your homework, you have discovered this. True, some quality is being traded for economy but this is your first time out of the chute, and even if a ton of money is available, you need to keep the cost of the game to a level where it can be given a competitive yet profitable retail price. Besides, the real quality of a game shows up in how it plays. How it looks is the perceived quality. People buy the game on perceived quality (the box top and bottom), but they enjoy it and, more importantly, recommend it to friends on the basis of how it plays.

When I was a kid we did not have a lot of money; like a lot of other kids. Toys - at least the store-bought kind – were pretty damn scarce in my house. Even then, the quality of your toys was not all-important. The play was the thing! I soon discovered I could use my cheap, opaque marbles to beat the pants of kids who had the fancy, expensive cat's eyes. Point made, I hope.

Basically, hundreds - possibly thousands – of man hours are saved when consumers punch out, gather and collate the various materials themselves. It really isn't all that bad, either. It gives the consumer a feeling of newness to punch out his own parts and something to do for ten minutes while the rules are read.

Back to tolerance. While the art is being done and the cards or money are being pasted down to their respective master sheets, check to make sure there is a one-eighth inch tolerance between the print image areas of each piece. It's cheaper to plan on these tolerance borders being white. An overlay to create a consistent color around the individual pieces can be prepared, but it will cost more because of bleeding.

Bleeding... Again, Not What You Think

The term 'bleeding' in graphics talk simply means that a color (or colors) is extended beyond the normal image area so that when the sheet is trimmed the color runs all the way to the edge. Jobs that bleed take more paper than jobs that don't, use more ink (which isn't cheap) and cost a little more to strip and print. In short, try to avoid costly bleeding when making components, but the extra investment may be worth it for your gameboard label.

The art for rules is virtually all typesetting and paste-up work, so there is absolutely no reason to get fancy here. If the length of the rules runs to more than four pages, they probably will have to be saddle-stitched, or stapled on the fold like a thin magazine. That does not cost too much.

Rules of the Game

There are two, critically important things to be sure of with respect to the rules. First, be certain to include as many easy-to-follow illustrated examples as are needed. Second, proofread them until you either need new glasses, or a new prescription for your old ones! A couple of bad typographical errors (called typos) or a dropped line in a set of rules, can ruin an otherwise great game and make it fit only for lining the cat's litter box. Regarding typos, like unused coat hangers in a closet they breed at night. I've seen six people proofread a set of rules, get them back after corrections, proofread them again, get them back after more corrections and proofread them a third time only to find new typos in the last set of corrections. Don't be upset when they're found. Be glad. When proofing something for the third or fourth time, there is a tendency not to really see the type. Force yourself to read one word at a time. THERE IS NO SUBSTITUTE. It is never safe to assume any correction has been made that hasn't created another, different typo.

Proofreading; Boring, but Essential

Proofreading is difficult, eye-straining, and boring.Your artist will snarl every time you find another error. But it must be done ... until everything is perfect.

It's impossible to describe every component a game might have, for it depends on the game. Most printed components fall into one of the categories described earlier. For a special piece, such as a wheel with a spinner, or a slide rule type affair, make a working prototype and take it to the artist on the first trip. If he doesn't know who can make it locally, take it to some printers and ask them. If you still can't get an answer, alter the component to something that can be produced locally. As a rule of thumb, if a game requires a custom made piece, have it made locally where a close watch can be kept on its progress. If standard pieces are to be used it's fairly safe to obtain them from whatever you consider to be the best source, regardless of location.

So far we've discussed the artwork, or the printed materials for the game. The next step is to discuss other items that aren't printed, that must be manufactured in a different manner.

COMPONENTS

While the artist is busy finishing the art and in between proofreading battles, try to find sources for the other components. Dice, playing pieces or pawns, colored chips, marbles and miniature silver camels' eggs are some of the most common pieces that are readily available. (Just joking about the camels' eggs.) You'd be surprised at what some manufacturers stock as standard items, though. If you're looking for something standard, the prices are usually reasonable and shipping dates are good.

To save you time and frustration, several trade magazines publish annual directories of toy and game manufacturers. By obtaining one or more of these directories, you'll find yourself with a 'who's who' of firms providing the industry with a full range of services and products. Though none will list every manufacturer in the world, I'd recommend contacting *Playthings Magazine* at Geyer-McAllister Company (51 Madison Avenue, New York, N.Y. 10010); their directory seems the most complete. Check local sources in the Yellow Pages also, and ask some printers.

Try to Avoid Customized Pieces

Above all, make every effort to stay clear of customized pieces. You can go bankrupt trying to produce them. Injection plastic molds simply are not cheap. The lowest price I've ever been quoted was $4,000 for a very basic piece ... and that was way back in 1981. Metal pieces tend to have less expensive mold costs, but the per unit cost for producing them will make you sweat blood. Besides, you need to be very careful about lead content in the pieces or you are going to be sued, get into trouble with government agencies, and have the game yanked right off the market. If a game requires a special piece that can't be bought or substituted by a standard item, go back to the drawing board to find a way around it. If the piece is absolutely essential, figure a way to do it through printing. It may be that by printing the necessary image on a sheet laminated to a cardboard (thick stuff, not what you get back from the laundry) and then die-cutting it into whatever shape you need, you'll wind up with the same effect for less money. Then, if the game does become a million-dollar seller, you can always go back to the original idea in a reprint.

There are some genuine horror stories involving inexperienced people who decided to have custom made pieces produced for games and handled it themselves. One of the worst tales is about a fellow who wanted two vacuum formed trays to fit in a game box. When delivered they not only didn't fit but wound up costing twice as much as he was led to believe. He was to receive 25,000 sets of these trays; instead, he got only 23,000. When he questioned the manufacturer he was informed they worked on a plus or minus 10% margin and they would not run their machines to produce the difference. This meant the poor fellow cold only assemble and sell 23,000 games even though he'd paid for components for 25,000, causing him to lose over $36,000 in sales – all the potential profits of the venture.

THE LURE OF THE ORIENT

At some point you will discover the economic advantages of having components produced in the Orient. True, if the quantity is large enough you'll not find a better price in this solar system, but BUYER BEWARE. There are more horror stories being told about Oriental production than you would believe. For the most part they center on ordering one level of quality, paying by letter of credit, then receiving lesser quality parts, parts of the wrong colors, or nothing at all until three months after the promised delivery date.

Buyer Beware!

A first hand example of this was a client of mine who ordered some customized plastic parts from Hong Kong. The price was better than the best American price by a full 25% and delivery was promised within sixteen weeks, which was a little longer than the twelve week American schedule. Ten weeks later, during marketing planning, my client called his Hong Kong factory to confirm the arrival dates and was told they might even ship early but not to count on it for advertisement planning. Armed with that information, the marketing and sales forces went to work. They obtained full page color ads in a very prestigious and expensive magazine, then informed some select department stores that their names would be listed in the ads if they purchased a certain number of games. The plan worked so well that all the targeted sales were made within two weeks. The ads were sent to the magazine, the space paid for and all that remained was to sit back and wait. My client had been clever enough to allow four weeks' tolerance between the date the plastics were supposed to arrive and the date the ads were to appear.

When the week of delivery rolled around the client called to ensure that everything was on schedule. "No problem," he was told by the voice thousands of miles away, that he'd never met. "Everything is on schedule."

It wasn't. To make a long story short the items weren't produced, let alone shipped, until 20 days before the first ads appeared. Shipping them via surface routing (e.g., ocean freight), the least expensive method, would place them in a U.S. port within a minimum of six weeks. The client had no choice but to air freight the shipment, to hold his orders and maintain credibility with the buyers. His

Hong Kong friends told him, "No problem. We have a relative who will ship for half what the airlines charge – just bring a check to the airport when they arrive."

A week later the local airport called and informed my client that his container had arrived and had been processed through customs. He could come pick it up, or have it delivered as soon as he brought a check for $18,000 to the office. As it turned out, $18,000 was about nine times the amount budgeted for surface freight cost and more than enough to throw the whole project into the red.

Of course, not everyone who deals with the Orient has these kinds of problems. A good rule to live by, if you are going to have parts or items manufactured in Hong Kong, Singapore, Taiwan, etc., is to plan to oversee the process personally, from the time the parts start rolling off the production lines to when they are put on the ship and sail eastward.

ARRANGING YOUR OWN FINANCING

Now that the creative work is done and you have finished shopping for playing pieces it's time to get down to business; to go to the bank, and then to visit a friendly printer. Let's talk about the banker first, since he'll provide you with leverage in your dealings with the printer.

At the bank, open up either an interest bearing savings account or a short term certificate of deposit that carries only minimal penalties for early withdrawal. Talk to a bank officer and tell him the account has been opened specifically to provide funds for a game project. He might raise an eyebrow, but he'll be happy to have the money and even happier that you didn't come to see him to borrow the funds for your (to his way of thinking) harebrained scheme. Inform him that you will be calling in the near future for a letter of credit, payable to a local printer upon your authorization.

Letter of Credit

The strategy behind securing a letter of credit is two-fold. Let's say you own a local company which will stake the game project. Unless it has an AAAAA credit rating – enough to convince the printer to stick his neck out and bill you for the work, that printer is going to want a good portion, if not all, of his payment up front. I'm not saying he's wrong. I've been in this business long enough to have seen many printers who didn't cover themselves financially get burned, and wind up writing the whole thing off as a loss. Remember, it may be your first encounter producing a game but it's almost certain the printer has had a number of undercapitalized people approach him with a game that was so big and gee whiz, just a heck of a lot of fun, etc. In short, a printer who is worth his salt and who doesn't know you from Adam simply is not going to get involved in a project without financial security. Why should he? He'd be the one taking all he risks!

The second reason for opening the bank account is so that you can provide yourself with some protection. By using the letter of credit form of payment, the printer is guaranteed his money when the job is delivered, and you're guaranteed that the printer is not going to take half of the money in advance and then proceed to produce the game at his own whenever-I-can-work-it-in pace. Another important accomplishment achieved by a letter of credit is that it establishes instant credibility with the printer. When he sees the LC, he'll know you are serious. He will quote or estimate the cost of the job more quickly, as well as being more willing to work with you to get the best job done at the best price.

VENTURE CAPITAL

I assumed, in the previous section, that you have the money to produce your own game, or at least enough real assets to provide collateral for a loan. What if you don't? You almost certainly won't get an unsecured loan from a banker. So, where do you get it?

Most people, you'll be relieved to know, don't have the funds to produce and market their own projects. Marketing money for games is often more important than money for production and it's got to be raised somewhere. Friends and relatives are often enticed into becoming investors, but this in itself is risky and really should be your last resort, since the odds are the friendship or family will split up over the project whether it succeeds or fails. If you decide not to test your personal relationships, give the world of venture capitalism a try and you'll quickly learn the real value of money.

Venture capitalists are groups or individuals who have money – enough money that they are able to invest in the sane financial arena and still have a little left over to try some crazy idea that might make them even richer. They don't usually have any desire to work in the companies in which they invest, but often they do demand a substantial — sometimes a controlling — interest in those companies.

Giving Up a Piece of the Business

How much control will they expect? Since venture capitalists know they are the last hope they tend to be demanding in their terms. If a project looks as though it has genuine potential and, equally important, they are impressed by the people behind the project, you will have captured their attention ... but not yet their money. If they are going to back you, they will insist on a substantial chunk of the project. When computing how much of the profits the inventor is to keep, normally the venture capitalist will ask to see documentation of the amount of actual money that has been spent to date (the inventor's time to this point has no bearing). Take the proven cash outlay, multiply it by 1.5, then figure the results as a percentage of the amount of the venture capitalist's investment. For example, if the inventor had a cash outlay of $10,000 the result when multiplied 1.5 times would be $15,000. If the capitalist is asked to put up $100,000, then the inventor would be allowed to keep 15% of the business.

Seems pretty steep, doesn't it? Not every deal is so hard but the above example is not unusual.

How to Find Venturesome Venture Capitalists

It's not as difficult as you might think. The first step in the process is to ask around. Investors in stocks, bonds and real estate are often approached by venture capitalist brokers – people who try to match individuals with ideas together with those who have money. You may even find a venture capitalist or a broker by simply asking friends or relatives.

Newspaper classified ads usually have sections listing the names of people seeking investors and those looking to invest. Making the right connection may be as simple as buying a few Sunday morning papers.

The business department of your local library can also prove invaluable in your search, for it contains references that classify types of businesses in a specific state, by county and city. Venture capital firms and bankers are everywhere. Finding them isn't really the hard part. The difficulty lies in getting them to say "yes."

One shark to be wary of is the venture capital broker who, for a small fortune, will put you in the same room with an interested party who supposedly has enough money to finance your project. The catch: you won't be told anything about the money connection before the meeting, but you will have to pay the fee up front, in advance; no refunds, no guarantees, thank you very much. I often have wondered just who is put in the room with you. Do people pay thousands of dollars to make a presentation to the broker's charming brother-in-law?

THE BUSINESS PLAN

The business plan, or prospectus, is one of the most essential tools for attracting investors. As such, it must be professional and highly informative.

A good prospectus is hard to find. There are people who make their livings writing such plans and they are paid handsomely for doing so. Once you try your hand at it you'll understand why. It's a lot of work.

Before getting down to the job of writing you should look at a completed prospectus, hopefully a good one. Check in the business section of your local library for books on how to write business proposals; reading one or two would go a long way towards helping to make your own plan successful.

After reading up on the subject you still have a tremendous amount of pre-writing preparation to do. From both the inventor's and investor's points of view, the two most important issues that will require immediate attention are marketing and management.

The marketing section of your proposal should detail the following: how the product will be sold and to whom; who will be doing the selling; when will the selling and buying take place; when and where the ads and promotions will appear and how much will they cost. In short, you need to create a real plan, one that is businesslike and attainable.

I have a friend who is an investment banker, a venture capitalist. He once said there are three kinds of business plans. The first kind (eighty percent are in this category) is put together to raise money, then tossed in the trash bin when the money has been obtained.Fifteen percent were prepared as a formality, to raise money that was already available. Only five percent were not only used to raise money, they were also real business plans – full of strategies and tactics, outlines and guides, benchmarks and jumping-off points — all the stuff used to put and keep a business on course. That's the kind of plan you want to put together.

The Management Team

The management team is your second important consideration. Potential investors want to be assured that the people who will be running the day-to-day activities of the new company will have the talent, ability, expertise and determination necessary to provide a good chance for success. Never offer to work for the company for nothing the first few years. Investors don't expect this and the idea is totally ludicrous. If the investors are interested they will expect to pay a reasonable salary to those behind the idea.

The management section should also include the names of the specific consultants or firms that are likely to be contracted in some capacity. For example, you'll be using graphic artists, printers, plastics manufacturers and maybe even some marketing and advertising consultants. All these people should be mentioned in your list of involved parties.

The Presentation

At times I have been hired to take part in presentations to groups of venture capitalists. I call these little get-togethers "shark feeds" and wouldn't attend one without being paid, and paid well. Sometimes these are bearable, almost pleasant events, but more often they are grueling sessions with the potential investors behind the bright lights and you under them.

When attending one of these meetings make sure you know your business plan inside out and be prepared to back up every statistic in it. If there's a fly in the ointment these guys will find it, but that's their job so try not to become defensive if the questions get petty. Often they are just trying to prove they know as much about the business plan as you do.

It's also an excellent idea not to face these financial wild cards alone. Bring as many of your experts as will come, for the more people you can be produce to demonstrate interest in the project, the more credible it will appear.

At the meetings just be yourself. Let your potential partners see the real you. If they choose to invest, you'll be seeing a good bit of each other and you should establish an honest, open relationship from the very beginning. Besides, these guys can spot every phony in Texas Stadium during the playoff games; you're not about to fool them so just act natural. If things go right you'll get your financial backing and you'll be ready to start your business. The next step will be to go see some printers. Since a number already have been contacted and your artwork produced to fit their standard sizes, the list should not take too long to complete.

VISITING THE PRINTERS

Dear Flabby,

I have a problem. I have two brothers: one is a printer and the other is a three-time loser on death row. I am going with a sweet young tattoo artist I met at reform school. We have so many pleasures in common, from full contact karate to swiping hub caps. I know we are perfect for one another. My problem is, I really love the guy and don't want to lose him, so should I tell him about my brother, the printer?

* * * * *

Printers are just like other businessmen. They range from scam artists – and worse – to those whom God Himself would hire to print His brochures, if He had any. The artist you select probably will be able to recommend one or more printers to you, and one of these might be right for the project. But remember the graphic arts business can be an "I'll scratch your back if you'll scratch mine" – just like any other business. The odds are the recommended printer will be a good one, capable of working effectively with your artist, but be careful; there are many capable printers who don't know beans about taking a game from start to finish. Don't rely only on your artist's recommendations. Make some inquiries yourself. Satisfy yourself that the printer selected can do the job. After all, it's your game – and your money.

Check Recommendations

After getting recommendations and checking them out carefully, narrow down your list of potential printers to three or so. Then call them and ask to speak to a salesperson. More than likely you'll have to leave a message and wait for someone to return your call. This is a good sign, for it means the company's sales people are out selling, which means the company is busy, which in turn usually means the company is a good one.

When the sales person calls back, simply tell him about your project. Inform him that the artwork is finished and that you would like to make an appointment to see him at his office. This last part is important. You are going to be spending a lot of money and you deserve a chance to see the plant where the work will be done. If the salesman says it would be more convenient for him to come to you, tell him to pick another time as you really would like to see his operation. If the salesperson still persists in visiting you instead, tell him you have to go and call the next name on your list. Don't start out by dealing with someone who is either ashamed of his plant or who is really a broker with no plant of his own at all.

Bring all your statistics with you to these appointments. In addition, have your itemized list of components with you for reference, so that you can quickly tick off your requirements, such as: the number and size of each part; the number of colors involved; instructions on bleeding; the type of paper to be used and the finish on it – whether trimmed, die-cut, folded or perforated. Impress upon these people the fact that you know your game thoroughly and demonstrate your seriousness about this project.

There's a good chance, regardless of how much you've learned so far, that some questions will be asked that you won't understand. Don't worry about it. Use these questions to educate yourself. Ask for explanations in laymen's terms. It's amazing how some printing salespeople can warm up to explaining their craft if they think someone is genuinely interested. If the conversation is still beyond your understanding, simply ask to see samples of what's being described.

At several points during these interviews you'll be tempted to turn the conversation to the subject of money. Don't! First of all, any figure at this point would be meaningless, for estimates involve much more than mere guesswork. They are exacting and tedious to do, and always take at least a couple of days. To help keep the cost as low as possible be sure to emphasize the flexibility of the game's components, relaying the sizes of those that can be made smaller in order to allow them to be ganged with one another.

The Importance of Ganging

Ganging simply means printing two or more jobs that share common colors and paper stock, on the same sheet. For example, a game may utilize two different decks of cards. They may be of different sizes and have different printings on their fronts and backs but if they are printed by four-color process on the same type of paper, and are the right size to fit the printer's press, they can be combined into one set of negatives, plates and press run. This will save you a considerable amount of money compared to printing them all as separate items.

Make sure people understand you know about ganging and want the printer to use it wherever possible; the more ganged, the more saved. In some cases a printer may try to talk you out of this. When ganging two or more four-color illustrations on the same sheet, for instance, a certain amount of color accuracy may be lost, because the correction of one color while the job is on the press does tend to throw off another color. If the printer mentions this, it's not necessarily because he's trying to get more money. Rather, it's because he can't tell how critical you are going to be about the final job. That's something we should discuss at this point.

Paying for Quality Control

I work with a company that prints everything from el cheapo, one-color placemats for fast food restaurants to limited edition, fine art prints sold through galleries for hundreds of dollars. The range of quality between these two extremes is like night and day. The fine art prints have to be perfect, with every nuance of color an exact match of the original. The placemats, on the other hand, have a limited purpose. They are to be used and discarded. The purchasers of the placemats see no reason to pay extra to insure that each one is exactly the same as the others. Next time you're in a restaurant take note of several placemats. You won't be able to tell the difference between them because you're only seeing a few at a time. They'll look good for what they are. If you saw thousands of them at the same time they'd still look good but you'd be able to spot slight variations in color. Some would be darker than others and so forth. The point is, any game is going to fall somewhere between these two extremes. You won't want the printing to be so poor that no two box wraps will look the same; on the other hand, you won't need, and shouldn't pay for, the exact repetition of a limited edition fine art print. Games aren't framed and hung for scrutiny. They are kept in closets and taken out occasionally to be played. Once the customer has removed the shrink wrap, the box is going to become soiled and scratched. So, if there is more than one piece of four-color printing that can be ganged, inform the printer you're aware of the problems with color correction but are not overly concerned with perfect matches. You just want the job to look good and the colors to be consistent.

While you are itching to ask how much everything is going to cost, the printer is trying to figure out the most tactful way to bring up the subject of money. He will typically want at least half in advance when he is actually ready to begin the work, with the balance payable on delivery.

Cost Estimates If a particular printer routinely does game projects, he may charge a fee of a hundred dollars or so to cover the cost of his estimate, although normally there is no charge for figuring commercial printing jobs. Most people are as ignorant of the costs involved in making their game as they are of the amount of work that goes into doing estimates. When they are told there is a charge, they usually beat a hasty retreat and the printer is out the salary of one or more estimators for a day or two. If the printer has a reputation for making games there's a good chance he gets several requests a week for estimates. If he didn't cover himself he'd be paying an estimator to spend all his time quoting prices for items that never got printed. Consequently, to save himself money and to weed out the amateurs, he charges a small fee to cover the cost of his estimator's time. That amount is eventually applied toward the total bill when and if he gets the printing job. Don't be suspicious of these fees, or resent them. It probably means the printer knows what he's doing and will have enough expertise to save you a lot of time, frustration, and money later on.

Exactly what is the printer going to do for you? The answer is as much as you want done and as much as you are willing to pay for. Some printers (a very few) will do a game from start to finish, including the art work. When the bill is paid and the games ready to be picked up, they are assembled, boxed, shrink wrapped, packed in shipping boxes and all set to sell. In other cases, at your option, you may choose to collect the printed items yourself and take them around to the various vendors who will make them into boxes, boards, card decks, rule books and whatever else you need. Then you are going to have to retrieve these pieces as they are finished and take them to wherever the games are to be assembled, where each piece will be left gathering dust until the last item arrives. Then they will be assembled and shrink wrapped.

If the game is handled this latter way, it increases the chances of errors and substitutes your time and labor for the printer's. If at all possible it's best to provide the printer with all the artwork, then let him handle everything else, from doing the four-color process separations to providing the finished products ready to ship. It's best for a couple of reasons. One, it becomes the printer's responsibility to make certain that everything is the right size and arrives on time; two, it frees you for the more important task of marketing. You will develop enough headaches from trying to sell the game; you don't need to lose sleep worrying whether about the box wrap fitting the box, or the board fitting in the box and the box fitting in the carton.

Catching Typographical Errors

While we're on the subject of responsibility, be aware that the printer is not responsible for proof reading and catching typographical errors. He'll provide several proofs before the job actually goes to press. There will be brownlines, color keys, and all types of camera-produced sheets to examine. They are not being done to squeeze extra dollars from your budget. The printer does them for self-preservation. It is your responsibility to catch the errors. The printer won't print anything until you've approved the proofs and signed them to show that you have examined them thoroughly. So, proofread everything and measure everything; don't assume that anything is right until you've done so. Once approved and printed it's too late. You've bought it!

When the subject of money comes up, make your position clear. Explain that you've opened an escrow account at a bank and that a letter will be drawn up guaranteeing payment upon delivery. If the printer isn't satisfied with this arrangement, go elsewhere. Remember, it's going to take between 45 and 90 days to complete the game and there's no point in your losing interest on your money during this time.

Unless you discover a printer you can trust right off the bat, try to get no less than three estimates. If one of the printers has a reputation for producing games and the others involved in the bidding don't, the odds are the experienced printer's bid will be slightly higher than the other two. If the difference is not over ten percent, consider letting him do the job because of his expertise. Unfortunately, there are some printers, as in every profession, who are less than honest. They will take an unsuspecting individual who is not familiar with the game industry, give him an exceptionally low bid to get the job, and later try to inflate the price once the work is half completed. If you get several quotes and one of them is substantially lower than the others, a little suspicion might be in order and a little additional checking on the printer's history might be required.

A final word for those brave souls who intend to try and save a little extra cash by handling each phase of their game's production. If you aren't content to let the printer do the entire job for you, it's entirely possible that you'll get by with what you've learned in this book, but you'll be a lot better off if, in addition, you read at least one book on printing and another on box making. You should also plan on spending a lot more time on the project – during normal business hours – than you might expect, for this is when the trade shops are open.

Time doing what? First, you'll have to run around to several box makers, scheduling appointments with each of them as you did with the printers. It's best to select the printer first so that they can coordinate dimensions. After deciding on a box maker, find someone to fabricate the gameboard. These people take a thick piece of cardboard, glue a piece of black paper to one side of it, neatly wrap the edges of the paper around the edge of the board, and then glue a printed game board sheet to the other side. This will be one of the most expensive items in the game. When trying to find a company to do this, make sure they have a laminating machine capable of doing the work. If they are planning on doing it by hand and are producing more than 2,000 games, you probably will find that you won't be satisfied with either the cost, the time factor or the degree of accuracy.

Shipping Cartons

Once your people are lined up and coordinated, find someone to make the corrugated shipping cartons, so you won't have to scrounge around your neighborhood grocery stores every night. Next, find someone to assemble and shrink wrap the game. If doing 2500 games or less, consider buying a cheap set of shrink-wrap equipment and do the job yourself, provided you have enough space to receive and store all the components until they can be assembled. Remember, an empty game box takes up the same amount of room as a full one, so until all the components are assembled and boxed, they'll need approximately twice as much room to store.

If all this can be faced cheerfully and you can stand singing favorite old songs while assembling mountains you'd swear were growing rather than diminishing, going this route will certainly save you some money in the short run. It's going to cost more in the long term, however, because you could have been, and should have been, spending all that time on marketing – the activity that really matters.

A WORD ABOUT CARD GAMES

If the game you're thinking of doing is a card game – one comprised of cards, a sheet of rules and a package – the road becomes at once simple, yet difficult.

It's simplified because of the few components involved and the relative ease of locating vendors of these components. Generally, your production costs should be far lower than if you had produced a full-blown boardgame. When your requirements are simple playing cards that must be shuffled and dealt frequently, it isn't difficult at all to find the names of various manufacturers in directories or business references.

Competition Is Tough

Difficulties will arise in being able to market your game competitively against the makers of, say, thousands of decks of cards at a time, whose economy of scale will enable them to retail a single deck at a price equal to what you would have to pay to have one deck produced. To add to your frustration, you should realize that the people who can produce the kind of playing cards you will need are the same competitors you will have to face in the retail market. They are the very firms with the equipment necessary for economically printing, round corner cutting, collating and plastic wrapping a deck of cards. They are the very firms, in short, engaged in producing and selling card games in the market place. Oh, they'll do it for other firms, sure, but somehow the price, regardless of quantity, never seems to be competitive with their own products.

It's also a little inconvenient that many of these firms are limited as to the size and number of cards they can produce per deck. When dealing with them make sure to ask for specifications early on in your discussions. If your requirements are 90 cards per deck but the equipment only makes decks in amounts of 56, then something has to change.

On the other hand, if your card game uses 'draw' cards, those which are left in a deck to be drawn and played one at a time, they probably won't need to be round cornered, plastic coated and shrink wrapped into individual decks. In this case, it should be easy to locate firms with machines known as card slitters and collators. They provide a broad range of sizes and numbers of cards in individual decks.

Since we've pretty much established that a card game from a new company can't compete head-on with the card game giants, it becomes necessary to compete on levels other than price. Packaging becomes more paramount than ever. The independently-produced game has to sell for more and it has to look like it is worth more; in other words, it becomes necessary to sell the sizzle, not the steak.

Your game may be far better than anything the big companies have on the shelves and it may be worth more money, but the consumers seeing the item for the first time won't know this. All they'll notice is that one card game sells for $1.99 and the other one for $7.95. There has to be some discernible difference between the two, either in packaging or in the promise of the game itself to provide $7.95 worth of fun the first time it is played.

Specialty Markets   I have a client who produced a card game dealing with the housing industry, called CONSTRUCTION CHASE. It consists of two decks of 56 cards each, a set of rules and a cleverly designed box. You won't find it easily in normal card game outlets, however. The inventors decided, after listening to some very sage advice, not to attack the traditional markets but to concentrate on a specialty target – the construction/real estate market.

This just so happens to be one of the largest specialty markets, because of the number of firms and people engaged in the industry. The game sells for $10 and at last check was doing extremely well being sold to firms as a gift item and to retail and wholesale outlets that never carried games before. By the time the specialty market is exhausted the game will have had time to establish itself and then it may be possible to ease into the traditional markets with minimum fuss and bother.

The point is card games can and do work, and sometimes they work better in non-traditional, less competitive markets where they can command a higher price tag.

MAKING COMPUTER GAMES

There are some things in life I don't really regret doing but would never do again – for the promise of any amount of fame, fortune, or political power. One of these things is the attempted start-up of a computer software game company.

If an individual combines the talents of a genius computer programmer, a brilliant game designer, and a devilishly clever business person, then maybe – but only maybe – the computer game market holds more than empty promises. But if any of these talents is missing, that person is well advised to avoid this market completely.

Ten, even five, years ago, the computer software market was wide open. Existing companies could not obtain new programs fast enough to feed a voracious market. Everything was sold while it was new. Retail prices were spectacularly high, as were profit margins, and when hardware technology made an older program obsolete, it was easy enough to drop the old game from the line and replace it with a new one. It was great fun, a financial/technological roller coaster ride with enough thrills to keep everyone happy.

But the ride ended. Soon enough the market became glutted, littered with the debris of second rate software. The successful companies, those still around today, began to spend extravagantly on advertising for their newest products. Eventually, the market evolved into one dominated by spending; he who spent the most sold the most. But sometimes that spending turned out to disproportionate to the sales and revenues obtained ... and another company bit the dust.

Today the computer game market, like the boardgame market, is dominated by a few large firms who have managed to weather the storms; companies who consistently produce quality products supported by strong advertising budgets.

If the computer game market looks like an entrepreneurial challenge you would like to accept, you may want to give it a shot. However, if you don't have the funds to promote your game heavily, don't waste your time.

Still want to give it a try? Your game/program had better be first rate and your computer graphics state of the art (warning: last year's "state of the art" may well be passe this year). Remember the perceived value of the game is shaped in the consumer's mind during the first few minutes of playing time.

Packaging and Graphics

Software packaging and advertising graphics compete against a higher standard than most board games. Their quality must reflect this. Fortunately, there is still a substantial profit margin available once the product has been established. The software can support a hefty packaging expense. Remember, that other than the packaging all the customer is getting is a flat black disk.

Another concern is disk reproduction itself. The price of disks has come down substantially in the past few years, as has the cost of copying or duplicating. Experience demonstrates even the quality oriented firms have a relatively high rate of defective products. Fly-by-night companies who use the cheapest disks and copying services find themselves replacing disks faster than they can sell new ones. It pays to maintain – and pay for – quality.

Know Programming — or Your Programmer

One final word, before we move on to the critically important subject of marketing. The software business is full of barely adequate programmers; individuals who know just enough to pass themselves off as experts to those who are truly novices. Unless you can program at least a little and understand the language of this business, stay away from the software business. The odds are heavily stacked against you.

MARKETING

WARNING: Regardless of how difficult designing, financing and manufacturing a game seems, these chores are all a short fall off a log compared to marketing.

THE KEY TO SUCCESS

When I did my first game I was too consumed with my own ego and delight at seeing my gem in print, to give a thought to marketing. I labored under the naive belief that if a better mousetrap was built (which I felt I had done) people would automatically beat a path to my door. It never occurred to me that all the work I had put into designing the game and nursing the project through its various stages, would just be a portent of things to come, a mere trifle compared to the task of getting and keeping my game on the market.

My plans were quite sketchy, almost nonexistent in fact. Fortunately I had lived a clean life, however, and providence came to my rescue. It must have! Based on everything I've learned since those early days, nothing but Divine Intervention can be credited for saving me from total ruin.

My first game went against all the rules. I produced only a thousand copies, thus creating a cost per unit that prohibited the game from being competitive in stores. This, in turn, limited me to the direct mail market. The theme of the game was an obscure campaign from the American Civil War, which meant I was creating a limited interest item in a narrow market. I titled it, "The Seven Days' Battles", an idea that came to me within three seconds after the artist asked me what to put on the box. The box art itself was a bland mix of a black line drawing from a hundred-year-old magazine and an undistinguished cream colored background. In short, everything was wrong with the game, but I didn't realize it at the time.

I now know that I did it the hard way - managing and coordinating each component. Consequently, the printed box top label did not fit properly on the box top, the game board was just a hair too large for the box bottom, about a quarter of the die-cutting had to be thrown out because I hadn't left enough tolerance and the bargain dice I bought tended to soften and melt in temperatures over 80 degrees. I didn't falter, though. It was still a good product and soon, very soon, I knew people would be flocking to my garage door to find a copy of this game they had heard so much about.

Being too impatient to wait for the first printed copies I took a photograph of my prototype and made up a quarter page ad, which I sent along with a check to the *Civil War Times Illustrated* magazine. Because of the long lead time the ad did not appear for three months, but this was for the best as things turned out. The boxes, boards and playing pieces, which were being made by three different vendors, were almost three months late in completion. They wound up being delivered two days after I received my copy of the magazine, with the advertisement buried 90 pages into it.

A (Lucky) Success Story

I began assembling games frantically and packed them for mailing. When orders started arriving I was elated. Every day I went to the post office, picked up ten or more envelopes containing checks, went back home and shipped the wise people their games. I had some other ads scheduled to appear in various other magazines, but none of them were out yet. Anticipating seemingly endless sales - based on the fact that I'd sold nearly 400 copies through one ad alone - I seriously contemplated going into reprints.

When the other ads finally started appearing, the orders fell far short of my expectations. In fact, they fell far short of reaching the lowest level of my worst fears. The reason for this, I discovered later, was that I was getting what is considered normal response to mail order ads. My first ad had pulled enormous results because of blind luck. The issue of *Civil War Times Illustrated* in which it appeared had carried several lengthy articles on the Seven Days' Battles campaign and my orders resulted from the backlash.

Had it not been for this monumental stroke of luck I probably would never have gotten into the game business. As it was, fate took a hand. I had done nearly everything wrong (though at the time I would have told anyone how brilliant I was), paid virtually no attention to the advice I received and still managed to break into the business. If you pay advice to only one section in this book, it should be this one.

Since those shaky early days I have come to the realization that the only key to success is marketing. I have seen incredibly great games produced by individuals or small companies come into the market and vanish without a trace. Why? They probably believed as I did, that making the game was the big job and that the sales would take care of themselves. I have seen the most mediocre game produced by a persistent marketeer cut out a permanent niche in the marketplace simply because he knew how and where to sell his game.

PRICING

Before actually marketing a game, its selling price must be set. In order to do this, you must assess how much it is going to cost to produce. Let's get an idea of what we're dealing with by taking an hypothetical game from start to finish. Our scenario involves a fairly recent development in the game market itself.

Perceived Value is a Key

Home video and computer games have had a major impact on the sales of board games because of their popularity. At first the impact was negative. Everyone was spending their money on the cute little games with lit up monsters eating their way across a screen. As the novelty wore off, people returned to more traditional games and the video boom went into a rapid decline, leaving some positive backlash in its wake. When video games were the rage they weren't cheap, some costing as much as $40. This raised the perceived value of board games in the eyes of consumers. Before the fad, game manufacturers believed a price barrier existed, that no game would sell in the general market for over $10. Today - as substantiated by the likes of TRIVIAL PURSUIT - a well-made, high quality board game can sell for as much as a video game. The only catch is that the board game must be top quality, with the kind of packaging and presentation to sell as a gift item.

Getting back to our hypothetical game, let's look at that beauty. Good looking game board! Great looking box! Say, this art is pretty good too! Now, all the art and typesetting winds up costing at least

$1,500. Figure on another $1,000 for the four color separations and $1,200 for the stripping to get everything ready to be put on the press, and it looks like an initial investment of $3,700 without a single copy in sight. These are the set-up or prep charges. Some game companies amortize them over the initial print run, others spread them out over many more copies than are first printed, and still others don't amortize them at all, carrying them on their books as an asset instead. To get a realistic picture of what the game will actually cost to produce it's best to include these prep charges in the initial print run, thus making the initial run a million dollar question.

Make too many of these things and you could wind up eating them with ketchup. Make too few and the cost per game is going to be so high that it won't be profitable. This is a big decision, one that your basic marketing strategy will hinge on, so the future of your gaming empire is at stake already. Don't panic, though. Simply ask the printer for a quote on 2500, 5000 and 10,000 copies, with a reprint price for 5000. How can I advise you so glibly? Simple! All that's really required is a quote on three quantities for the initial run and a quote for reprints to eliminate any prep or set-up charges the second time around.

Initial Order Quantities

Unless you've had a recent windfall, you're probably not going to be able to afford much more than 10,000 copies of the game. At this level we're talking a minimum of $30,000, and that's assuming the game is pretty basic. Going down the scale, 5,000 copies of the game should cost $22,000, which would push the retail price up a bit. At the bottom of the barrel, 2500 copies will cost somewhere around $16,000; if you're going to try to wholesale the game to retailers, it will be difficult to eke a worthwhile profit out of so small a run. So why would anyone bother producing this minimal quantity? They'd do it because of the options involved. For the sake of this example, we'll assume this is the number of copies chosen.

First, we'll assign a retail price to the item high enough to ensure recovery of cost and expenses, yet low enough to be palatable to interested consumers. To go about this, we determine the raw cost per unit. In this case, it's $7.88 per game, if we include the $3700 spent on art work - pushing us over the retail price of some of the cheaper versions of mass market sellers.

With this kind of cost, we have to look on the limited run as a 'market test'. We're going to try to sell out as quickly as possible and hope to break even. There's just no way to wholesale (selling to stores and distributors who in turn retail to consumers) at this level and make a profit. This is because the price must be structured so as to allow the retailers to make a profit. I could have said fair profit, but if you're in the situation we're discussing you won't think there's anything fair about it. This means having a suggested retail price of $16 per game, a little high for the average mass-market game, but about right for a specialty item. When wholesaling the game, it will sell to stores at 50% off the retail price, or $8, plus freight charges. Almost all firms buying games get at least 50% off and 30 days in which to pay the bill. They usually get freight paid too, if they buy a large enough quantity.

Profit Analysis   Let's stop to look at our scenario so far. We've got 2500 games to sell at $8 apiece. Being super salespeople, we manage to do this quickly and the last items are shipped out 90 days after we've received them. Tack on another 30 days to collect all the money, estimating that about 10% of our customers are going to be late in paying, if at all, and we can anticipate a gross sales of $20,000. Not bad for 2500 copies, you may say, but now we have to start deducting. We said about 10% of the debt wouldn't be collected on time and maybe never, so subtract $2,000. Then, there are sales expenses for the cost of the sale. It's a good bet there weren't any television commercials but some money had to be spent no matter how good a salesperson you are. Remember – there were those advertising flyers that had to be printed. They were only in black and white but they cost around $80. And don't forget the art and type for them, which makes another $50. There were long-distance calls totaling nearly $1,000. Add on postage to mail the flyers, envelopes and the $200 charge for the mailing list and we're up to $1,600. There were probably some other expenses too, but for now this will be enough to make a point. We started out with $20,000 in sales, then we subtract:

        $ 2,000.00 for bad debts
        $ 1,600.00 sales expenses
        $16,400.00 gross profit.

Now subtract the $16,000 the games cost to begin with and you're lucky to be left with $400, which comes to a 3% return on your investment.

Notice there is absolutely no overhead figured into this. There's no money to pay neighborhood kids to ship the items. There's no mention of rental for warehouse space, utilities or transportation of the items from the printer's facilities to our own. These are all details requiring ingenuity, some child labor and a spouse's willingness to let us get this idea out of our system. In addition, we haven't figured on funds for travel, trade shows and conventions. So why are we bothering to do only 2500 copies?

Well, the low run would offer a couple of options. The first is being able to test the waters. At the end of it all we'll see how difficult it will be to sell out a small run and how long it will take. We'll also learn which stores are likely to come back for reorders. But, you say, we've done all this work, sold all these games and still have just about the same amount of money as when we first started. So what's the big deal? Well, we only had to sell 2500 copies, not 5000 or 10,000. If it took us a long time to sell this amount, how would it feel knowing there were still 7500 to go? Having sold the games, tested the market and recovered the investment, we can go on from there.

Reorder Quantity Options

If satisfied with the game's reception - i.e., everybody reordered within a week, sold out within a month and making money was never so easy - then we know to reprint the game and keep it on the market. After this experience we can gauge how many will be sold in a month's time and how many to reprint to start making a profit. It's important to keep a cool head, however, and not go gangbusters printing 100,000 copies and hiring scores of salespeople. Look to doing between 10,000 and 25,000 copies this time around. That will give us plenty of room to play around with price and profit, but not enough to supply every platoon of the Soviet Army with a copy just in case the sales quit on us.

Let's assume things went okay, but not great. All 2500 copies sold but it took a lot longer than expected. The second option is to reprint 5,000 or 10,000 copies and keep plugging away at the market place, but this time including a reasonable profit for our labors. Suppose we did all right, but we decided that it's just not worth the effort to keep at it. Now we have a published game that did sell, and this affords us yet another option: that of approaching big game companies.

That's right! Those same companies that wouldn't even open our letters before will possibly look at the game now because they won't be looking at just a game. They are going to be looking at somebody's published game, along with a marketing analysis covering sales on the first 2500 units over a six-month period. They are not going to worry about being sued for copyright infringement because the game has already been published and copyrighted. Consequently, they don't even have to worry about somebody filing a harassment suit in case the game is similar to their own. If we send off a crisp, professional letter and follow it up with a couple of phone calls, we should be able to persuade someone to at least look at the game. If we get an offer to buy the rights to it, we know we gave it our best shot and now can look forward to earning royalties while someone else takes over the sales.

The options obtained by producing only 2500 copies should appeal to the pessimist in us. What about the other quantities - 5,000 or 10,000? They offer the same options but with the added disadvantage of taking longer to sell out. To compensate for the longer selling period, they offer some advantages that couldn't be factored into the smaller run.

Let's take the 10,000 quantity first. We've already established a hypothetical cost of $3 per game at this level. We'll set a retail price of $12 instead of $16, to speed up sales. At this price we'll be getting $6 each from the retailers, and we'll still have room to pay freight costs if a buyer orders multiple items. We'll also have room for more sales expenses, so we can run an extra ad or two.

The bottom line shows us that since we've got four times as many units it's going to take us longer to move the games but, hopefully, not four times as long: after all, the lower retail price should help us. But the added time mans additional sales expenses.

Ten thousand copies at $3 each is $30,000 for the COG (cost of goods). Our expenditures are as follows:

Magazine Ads	$ 6,000.00
Long Distance Charges	$ 2,000.00
Shipping Charges Big Orders	$ 750.00
Direct Mail Printing, Mailings and Mailing Lists	$ 1,000.00
Bad Debts or Slow Pays	$ 6,000.00
TOTAL EXPENSES	$15,750.00.

Now, add in a COG of $30,000 and the total cost comes to $45,750. How'd we do? We sold 10,000 copies at $6 apiece for a total gross sales figure of $60,000, giving us a net profit of $14,250.

Not bad! That's a tidy sum in addition to our regular annual income and at the same time we've conducted a thorough test. At this point it will be easy to decide what to do next: whether to go on and make more games, contact major game companies or just drop the whole idea.

If you decide on a second run, you'll have to take care not to overextend yourself. The game market is a fickle place and it's important to remember that it takes about four years for the average game to reach a true market position. This means a four-year commitment on your part.

DO-IT-YOURSELF ADVERTISING

After you've armed yourself with the names, addresses and rates for special interest magazines appropriate to your game, start scheduling ads to appear after your game is ready to be shipped. Don't get too anxious. It's very important that the ads not appear before the games are ready. If possible, fill the orders the same day they arrive. You'll want your customers to think that both you and your company have got it all together. This may seem a little exaggerated, but it isn't. I've seen too many people turned off by having to wait for mail order items. By the time the order is filled, the customer has lost whatever interest he had in the first place.

Consumer Advertising

Spend a lot of time creating your ads. The headline, regardless of the size of the advertisement, has got to grab the reader's attention; if it doesn't, it's a cinch the rest of your copy won't be read. Look through some magazines for headlines, then cut out the ads and accumulate a bunch of them. Sort through them, making stacks of best, good and why-did-you-pick-them-in-the-first-place categories. Take notes on the best of the best and try to determine whether there's a possible tie-in with your own product. When you're finished you'll have a pretty good idea of how to make your own ad work.

Ad Copy and Layout

Once you've got the headline, do a sketch of an accompanying photograph of your game all laid out, with the box standing up behind the board and components. Then get started on the copy. Make it honest and upbeat and remember - you're doing it with pencil and paper, not chisel and stone. Don't be afraid to make changes. Touch on what you think people will want to know about the game, such as what it's about, is it easy to learn, who it's geared for and so on. Since it has to sell the game in much the same way as the box back, you may be able to use some of the same written material.

One way to go about this - the wrong way - is to say something like, "This game is about football. It's a lot of fun because people who like football will enjoy it. It's easy to learn and easy to play and everyone will want to. It sells for $12 and you can order it from the address below."

This little masterpiece certainly answers all the questions, but it falls short in creating enthusiasm or desire. We'll try it again, only this time with a little 'oomph'.

"The score is tied. The two-minute warning seems a lifetime ago. It's third down and six, your last chance to get in field goal range. The ball is snapped. The quarterback fades back as the defenders blitz. He side steps one tackler, ducks under another, firing a long pass down the side line. The receiver leaps to make the catch only to be hit on his way down. He bobbles the ball, holds on, breaks a tackle and heads down field. He's at the fifty, the forty, the thirty-five, he's....

You'll know all the excitement of professional football when you've played...JOCKO.

JOCKO! It's a new game for the armchair coach in all of us. Easy to learn, fast-paced to play, JOCKO creates the feeling of being on the gridiron as YOU make the decisions and YOU call the plays. No longer will you have to watch passively as your favorite team struggles against its arch rivals. In less time than it takes to watch a game, you'll actually play it. JOCKO! A great game for the whole family. It's available at better stores everywhere. Ask for it or order directly from us. This exciting new board game is yours for only $12. So come on, get out of those bleachers and onto the field. Place your order today."

This may not be perfect but it's a whole lot better than the first attempt. It represents only one type of approach. Once you've looked through a ton of magazines, you'll find many possible styles.

After settling on your ad and neatly typing it and marking it for headlines, in bold and italic type, make another run to the artist. He'll probably have to make some more changes, because people generally end up writing more copy than will fit comfortably in an ad. Then you'll have to do a rewrite. As long as the copy is being rewritten anyway, save yourself some time by instructing the artist to lay out the ad to run full, half and quarter-page size. It's a sure bet you won't be able to afford full page ads everywhere, but you should try to get as much mileage out of the typesetting as possible. Tell the artist how many copies of each size you'll need, so that everything will be ready to be picked up at once.

Trade Advertising   Once in the mail, forget about the consumer ads for a month or two, until they begin to appear, and start concentrating on another type of ad - for trade publications. These are magazines that are sent to people in a particular trade, in this case retailers and wholesalers. There are actually quite a few and their names and addresses can be found in directories at local libraries, or by asking toy and game merchants for back issues. Before starting to work on an ad for this group, you should understand a little about the way these people think.

First off, trade people buy and sell a lot of games. Hundreds of titles are thrown at them every year. They don't have the time or the inclination to study each and every one of them. If a game looks to be a big seller, they'll know about it before anybody else. If a game is a real dog, they'll know that too. But, if a game is new and doesn't really have a track record, they tend to base their decisions on the following factors: How does the package look? Will it attract attention and make people want to pick it up? Will the back of the box sell the game if someone reads it? How much advertising is behind it? What are the discounts and terms - is there enough profit involved to make it worth handling? (Sound familiar?)

Notice there's no mention of whether the game is fun to play or who's going to play it. These people aren't game playing experts; they are merchants. The only thing they are interested in is how fast they can sell this merchandise.

Obviously an advertisement that will gain attention in the trade publications must address specific marketing needs. It will require more pictures and less type. The copy should emphasize discounts, packaging and selling ability. If running ads in a well-known magazine, add a line saying, "As seen in Big Time Magazine", to create the illusion that there is a lot of advertising behind the game.

In reality, this will only be an illusion considering the cost of advertising. When one of the major companies promotes a game they spend upwards of twenty-five million dollars, but they do it for reasons other than one might expect.

Trade Shows   The first time I witnessed this ploy was at a trade show in Atlanta. There I was, sitting in my plain, cheaply outfitted eight-by-ten-foot booth across from the elaborate booth of an internationally known toy and game company. Talk about a deflated ego: their exhibit was worth more than my entire company. Anyway, they had an item the toy buyers were lining up to order, kind of a plastic tricycle or little kids. At one point the line was so long that it extended beyond their area and curved past mine. Quite a few of the buyers glanced disinterestedly at my limited line of wares while waiting to place orders with the other guy.

I struck up a conversation with one particularly friendly gentleman, and he showed me how advertising could work in the toy and game industry. It seemed this particular toy manufacturer had budgeted around thirty million dollars to promote his product on television during the coming Christmas season. The company had a big chart showing which channels would air the ads and in what cities. As a special favor to the firms that bought in large enough quantities, the manufacturer would let retailers plug their stores at the tail end of the commercials. You see this kind of thing all the time. A commercial comes on showing toasty brown young women drinking soda in an island setting and at the end a sign flashes on the screen saying, "Available at your neighborhood Ripo Grocery Store". These buyers were actually waiting in line to place orders in the amounts of thousands of dollars, and the man I'm talking to is telling me that it's such a good deal! Here, the toy manufacturer is selling items for $14 apiece and the stores in turn will sell them to customers for $13.95 and it's a bargain? This means the stores will lose a nickel on each item sold, doesn't it? What's going on here?

Loss Leaders

It's called a loss leader. The store owner buys the item for slightly more than he will sell it because all the advertising the manufacturer is buying in his city will attract people to his store; he is gambling that once someone comes into the store they are going to purchase something other than the advertised product.

Can you compete with that? Of course not, unless your game is so popular and in such demand that people are clamoring for it. Thankfully the major manufacturers usually do this with only one item during the holiday selling season.

Just as a side note, loss leaders are not confined to games and toys. Virtually all producers of consumer items who can afford to commit the advertising dollars do it every now and then, sometimes as a means of reducing their stock of slower-selling items. Fortunately they won't affect you too much initially since you won't be selling to very many major outlets in the beginning.

Back to the trade ads. Most magazines charge more for advertising space than might be expected, based on their circulation. The reason for this is simple. They are offering to send their magazine containing your ad to known buyers of a product category and their only real income is from the sale of ad space. In many cases the magazine itself is free.

The people who sell space for these publications do only that. They are hustlers (not in any dishonest sense), working hard to earn a living. Once they find out someone is in the market for trade space they can be relentless. Don't be persuaded to put all your eggs in one basket. Make it clear you have a limited budget, all of which has been committed, and you'll get back with them, based on the performance of the current series of ads. Don't be shy - they sure aren't.

Another aspect of trade publications is that they all have a new products section. This area of the magazine spotlights new items that may be of interest to buyers. Send a copy of your game to the magazine for inclusion in this section and you'll receive some free advertising space where you'll be able to show a picture of the box top, a line or two about the game, the name and address of your company, the suggested retail price and, in some cases, a reader service number. Reader service numbers, when they appear, are seen throughout the magazine. In the back of the publication there's a postage paid response card the reader can tear out to obtain additional information about the product, from the publisher. You receive a computerized printout with all this data, including the names and addresses of the companies who circled your number. You follow up these leads to create new customers for yourself. It's a good service and if you're going to be promoting your game in trade publications, you should take advantage of both the free publicity available in the new product section and the sales leads generated by the reader service card.

THE CIRCUIT

After the ads have been placed and the games warehoused it's time to get out there and push the product. Everyone else with a game on the market is sweating right alongside you to ensure that their product sells, so you can't afford to be different. I hope you enjoy traveling, because you are in for a good deal of it.

Your starting-off point may be the numerous boardgame conventions that are held for consumers. These tend to be small and are scattered around the country at different times during the year. Nearly all trade and game specialty magazines publish monthly calendars of the major conventions in addition to some minor ones. It's important to attend as many of these shows as possible during the first year of your game's life. This is one place to really get your word-of-mouth advertising started.

Boardgame Conventions

The people who attend these conventions are hard core gamesters. If they like a game and buy it, they'll start teaching their friends as soon as they get home. True, most of these conventions have a fantasy, science-fiction or military history theme, but I've seen major corporations in attendance more than once.

Go to these conventions with two aims in mind: demonstrate and sell. To demonstrate the game try running mini-tournaments where the rules are taught before each round. Copies of the game will serve as prizes. Be your most charming and personable, doing your best to get people really excited. Get them whooping and hollering over each throw of the dice. This will draw a crowd, which is exactly what you want. The more people who actually look at the game, the more you'll have a chance to sell. Speaking of which...

You should try to sell at least a few copies while at these conventions, not only for word-of-mouth purposes but also to help defray travel costs. Most of the time you'll be able to rent booth space and tables for a reasonable charge and if you can't recruit some free help, alternate between selling and running demonstrations. After a few of these exhibitions you are going to get really bored. You'll find yourself coming up with excuses for not attending any more shows. You should persevere, however, for conventions are the most concentrated way to show your game to lots of people.

Demonstration in Stores

I remember a game we produced a few years ago. It was a role playing game which was going into an over-saturated market against some well-entrenched competition. We had a promotions man who travelled around the country doing demonstrations in stores, like the Duncan Yo-Yo men of yesteryear. I foolishly volunteered to travel with him for a few weeks, helping with demonstrations. Each display involved running an adventure or scenario for four to ten players. Each episode lasted about three hours, unless the kids were really into it and having fun, and then it could run up to four or five hours. The problem was, it was always the same adventure. By the third time I'd done it, I knew fifty pages of the text by heart. By the tenth time I didn't even bother to take out the book. By the twentieth time I could do it while catching forty winks. I ran the same adventure nearly 200 times in about half as many days and I was so sick of it at the end of the tour that I wanted to burn all my personal copies of the game. But you know something, it worked!

A year later, when we looked at the sales statistics, we found that the game did better in the states where I did the demos than the states I hadn't visited. By my taking the time to demonstrate the game to 1,000 people, I sold an additional 5,000 copies that first year. So, don't negate the usefulness of demos. They are a powerful tool and once you feel comfortable with them you'll find it reflected in your sales.

After the conventions, your next target should be the retail outlets.

INDEPENDENT STORES

Most stores you'll deal with initially will be of the Mom & Pop variety; small owner-operated stores that are not part of a chain or franchise. There are literally thousands of these in the country, and you can obtain mailing lists for them that are broken down by type: i.e., toy, gift, game, hobby, etc. An essential facet of your marketing strategy should be to budget mailings of advertising flyers to as many of these outlets as you can afford. The only way to achieve the level of orders you'll need, however, is to stop in and see them, show them your game, talk to them and sell them right on the spot.

A couple of years ago I helped a lady from Texas produce a game. She was an extremely intelligent person but at the time she had zero knowledge of the game industry. I had considerable apprehensions, but we made the game and delivered it boxed and ready to ship.

Ignoring our advice, the lady went into action promptly. Her marketing strategy was basic but it turned out to be pretty irresistible. Her plan was herself. She jumped in body and soul, travelling to conventions, fairs, trade shows, art shows - you name it. Wherever there was any kind of gathering with a few hundred or a few thousand people in attendance, she was there. On the way to these events she would stop in every town she passed, check the yellow pages for the names and addresses of the local game and toy shops and then, as she put it, "boogie on in", taking a few copies of her game with her. As she traveled she sold her games daily, through sheer personal force. This one-woman tornado spent two years sweeping through Texas and Louisiana and the rest of the southwest before heading up to Colorado and California. Her initial sales just about covered the cost of her trips and she gained more and more exposure for her game with each new stop. Before too long reorders began to come in and it became obvious that her game was actually selling. It's not a big hit yet, but from the look of things it's going to be around for quite a while and it may turn into a real money-maker.

As far as I know this enterprising lady has spent less than $2,000 on all the advertising connected with her game, other than travel and direct sales expenses. Now you might not have the time to travel to this extent but the point is, this lady, using her inventory to pay for her trips, managed to carve out a niche in the marketplace, with only a little additional expense. One reason her method worked was because the game had continuous, escalating exposure; and the more people who hear about a product, the greater the potential for sales.

HOW TO GET EXPOSURE

Basically, there are three ways to gain exposure: you can buy it, work for it or have it thrust upon you.

1. Buying exposure means advertising. In the beginning this will be only the second most effective method, but by far the costliest. The outright buying of advertising space takes plenty of cash, but there are other ways.

   One possibility is to offer an extra discount to your retailers - say, 5% - in exchange for taking your game and making a window or aisle display, then sending you a photograph as proof. This works well because window displays are the equivalent of prime time television in retailing; once a retailer has gone to the trouble to set up the display you can bet it will stay there for a while.

   Another method is to hook up with one or more mail order houses and conduct what is known as "per inquiry" or P.I. sales. The mail order house places an advertisement for the game in its catalog, which is mailed to customers. As the orders and checks come in, half the money along with the names and addresses of the customers are passed on to you and you ship out the game. Sometimes it's difficult to convince mail order houses that they will get enough business from an item to make the ad worth their time and money but, if possible, this is a great way to create awareness of the product.

Free Publicity

2. The second way to gain exposure - working for it - is the most common route and one that you can do something about on a day-by-day basis. It involves, as has already been discussed, travel. There is absolutely no substitute. There is an alternative, though, that involves writing. Make a habit of typing a press

release at the end of every month. I know this sounds silly but if it's appropriate and timely it just may get published.

Let's say you're going to be travelling to Eureka, Arkansas for a convention. Send press releases to as many neighboring newspapers as possible, announcing that you are coming to demonstrate an exciting new game about (insert a brief description) at the convention, and give the date and location. Go on to mention how long the game has been on the market and how well it is doing. Conclude by telling everyone they are invited. The game may not be newsworthy - not yet, anyway - but the convention may be and the newspapers may have been aware of it. They might run the piece more to announce the convention than to plug your game but what difference does it make? You're still getting a plug.

Another way the written word may come in handy is if the game appeals to a specialized market. Those same magazines where you advertised may be ripe for an article telling how the game can be used to educated people about a particular issue. For example, suppose a game deals with highway construction and you found a magazine called ROADWORK TODAY. Write an article describing how your game teaches people the basic laws of building highways. If the item is fairly sophisticated, you might even market it as a model for planners and engineers.

Write an Article About Your Game

These articles must be more than thinly disguised advertisements, however. They must be newsworthy or, at the very least, something fun to read that a publication can perhaps use as a filler. Make sure to send copies of every press release to radio and television stations in addition to the print media. One group of enterprising game inventors actually had disc jockeys playing their game on the air on 12 radio stations around the country.

If the subject of the game is appropriate, send some press releases to college and university newspapers. These publications are generally more receptive and often seek offbeat articles. Besides, most people don't realize that TRIVIAL PURSUIT, PENTE, UNO and DUNGEONS & DRAGONS were all campus crazes before they hit the big time – another important advertising consideration. College campuses, especially dormitory ones, are a closed environment in many respects and word-of-mouth spreads much faster than it does out in the real world. College age people tend to be very enthusiastic about whatever they're into at the moment; if a game becomes the rage on campus there's a good chance the news will spread back home during the holidays.

Another group to keep in mind are the potential buyers. They should receive a copy of each press release as well as photocopies of each published article. This is a good way to keep the name of a game in front of them: eventually they won't remember whether they read the article in a magazine or off of a press release form, so even if many of the releases/stories don't get printed, their cumulative effect will still be the same with the buyers.

3. The third and most sought-after form of publicity, the kind that is thrust upon you, can only be obtained if and when a game gets really hot. With this kind of exposure you're home free.

Every now and then the media 'discovers' a new game that is sweeping the nation and everyone, from the Wall Street Journal to the Congressional Record, carries stories about it. Usually by the time this occurs the game is already several years old and the designer has retired to some South Sea island, having been bought out by a major game producer. If you ever do become a darling of the media, though, you're in for a wild time. Sales can increase ten or twenty fold virtually overnight. Unfortunately, the only way I know to obtain this kind of attention is to have pre-existing sales of a hundred thousand copies, with your game already being played by millions - or for you to temporarily buy out the game. Actually, this is what we did some years ago.

Do you recall the summer when the biggest question in the news was, "Who Shot J.R. Ewing?". We obtained the rights to do a game based on the television show, *Dallas*. It cost us a pretty penny of front money, but we also bought instant recognition. We threw a press party in Dallas, Texas that generated more media exposure than we could ever have afforded. As the season dragged on, however, and the mystery was solved, interest waned and so did the coverage. This is why I call it buying exposure temporarily.

PRESS RELEASES

There are two kinds of game-related press releases. One kind is short, to the point and serves as a space filler in magazines and newspapers, to keep a company's and/or product's names in front of potential customers. There are also the news story type press releases, written as though they were full-length articles. For purposes of clarity we'll refer to the first type as a press release and the second type as a story and together they'll create public relations, or PR.

As far as media people are concerned, press releases are like swarms of mosquitoes. In order to be noticed, a release has to stand out visually from all the others that arrive in the same batch of mail. A good idea might be to select a simple piece of graphics from the game itself, combine it with the logo type of the product and have it imprinted on some nice stationery. Choose colored stock, with type set letterhead and matching envelope, complemented by a contrasting color of ink. Make sure to include the words 'Press Release' in large type on the sheet. Print several thousand copies of these 'blank' letterheads. Then, as press releases are created, take them to the quick copy printer to have the news items printed on them from a typed sheet.

Stories, on the other hand, are written and submitted just as if a freelance writer were trying to get one published. Include a note on a press release form as a cover letter and hope the story is good enough to grab the attention of a staff writer. The story must be newsworthy. It should have some human interest appeal, or some local flavor, or be about some current hot topic. Here are a few sample headlines, and what the story might be about:

Hometown Postman Makes Game

Story to be sent to local newspapers and tells of retired postal employee turned game inventor: why he invented the game; what it's about, etc. Concentrate on human interest element.

Smallville Housewives Become Game Tycoons

To be sent to female oriented magazines and tells of housewives entering the game market: why they invented this particular game, what they did before, what is the game's market.

Cocaine Game Teaches Lesson

Tells about ex-cocaine addicts inventing game while in prison.

This last example may be dramatic but stories do need a little drama and excitement if they're to be noticed. Always consider the type of publication you're contacting and slant your story accordingly. Who should get releases? The following is a list of the types of media and publications to keep in mind.

Get Your Message to the Media

RADIO STATIONS - nationwide, but especially local talk shows and stations that may have an interest in interviewing a local inventor. Aim for talk stations as opposed to top forty stations. Send a sample sheet, if possible, describing how the game can be played on the air.

TELEVISION STATIONS - nationwide again, even though there seems little point in hoping that one of Mr. Carson's under assistants will select your game as the one to show the week after Thanksgiving. But you never know - and local early morning talk shows often need offbeat items and interesting people.

LOCAL PUBLICATIONS - newspapers and city magazines (i.e., Philadelphia, Atlanta, Chicago, Dallas, Houston). Slant stories for local flavor, perhaps comparing cities according to numbers of game inventors, markets, etc.

REGIONAL PUBLICATIONS - those covering a certain geographical area (i.e., *Texas Monthly, Ultra, Southwest Magazine, The New Englander, Florida Today*). Slant stories in much the same way as for city magazines but with more regional flavor.

NATIONAL PUBLICATIONS - this is the big league (i.e., *Time, Newsweek, U.S. News & World Report, Redbook, Cosmopolitan, Vogue, USA Today, The Wall Street Journal*). These publications usually carry stories on an item that has remained hot for a prolonged period of time.

TRADE/INDUSTRY MAGAZINES - periodicals that cover specific industries, hobbies or events related to the subject of the game.

POTENTIAL BUYERS - A thorough list should be created and maintained of every potential buyer and each should receive a copy of the press release as story as they are submitted or published.

PRESS AGENTS/PR FIRMS

A good press agent or public relations consultant can generate more publicity than can normally be purchased for ten to twenty times the amount of their fee. Just make sure you fully understand the rate schedule and all the conditions.

Agents and PR people seem to come in two flavors - either print or electronic media. The very large agencies certainly have the ability to cover both but they usually charge more than smaller ones. The latter (some are individuals operating from their homes) tend to be less expensive but may be limited in terms of experience or ability. For example, a particular agent may be familiar with regional newspapers and magazines but have virtually no worthwhile contacts in radio or television. In the beginning it's best to stick with someone whose primary talents are in print, because of the expense involved. Should you have enough funds to cover both print and the electronic media be sure to hire someone with the ability to set up and book an interview tour. This consists of sending a game inventor around the country, scheduling appearances on local talk shows. Since you'll be traveling to conventions anyway, there's a chance the trips can be combined.

PRODUCT TIE-INS

One thing leads to another. A client of mine was reading a trade magazine looking for new outlets for her game when she came across an article about an upcoming anti-illiteracy campaign sponsored by some heavyweight organizations. Since her product was a word game that fostered literacy (though somewhat indirectly) she saw a tie-in. She sent the game along with a letter to the campaign headquarters, and several phone calls and meetings later her game was officially sanctioned by the campaign and its sponsors. This generated immediate sales activity, as associate member organizations learned of the product through conferences and newsletters. The game was made more credible because of its official connection with such a noble cause, so my client went off hunting elephants. She convinced a nationwide fast food chain to try a version of her game on their paper placemats, with a blurb supporting the anti-illiteracy campaign. The test went extremely well; the fast food chain commissioned a variety of placemats using the game and paid the inventor a royalty. Thus, this imaginative lady managed to put herself in the position of being paid to promote her product. Tie-ins often involve licenses but this case is a perfect example of one that made rather than cost money.

At this point we have to change course and take a closer look at potential marketing areas.

GAME MARKETS

There are six basic markets for a game: the traditional toy and game market, educational, book, gift, stationery and specialty markets. Each of these can be broken down further into four sub-markets: direct sales, independent retail outlets, wholesalers and chain stores, premium/incentive buying. The groupings are defined as followed, although there may be some cross-over (a school library, for instance, might fall in both the educational and book markets).

1. Traditional Toy/game Market.

Retail stores and wholesalers who generally carry popular games on a year-round basis.

This is normally the largest potential market for games. It is comprised of every type of store or distributor with games on their shelves year-round, ranging from the Mom & Pop stores to mass merchandisers like K-Mart, Toys-R-Us or Sear's. The mass merchandisers are the ones with the ability to put your game in the big leagues. Unfortunately, they tend to be interested only in games that are proven winners, with a ton of advertising money behind them, that are offered by major manufacturers. If you're able to break into this market, you'll have the advantage of selling high volume to solid companies certain to pay for the goods. The disadvantages you'll find are that you'll have to work like the devil to get into this market and then you'll virtually have to give your product away. You'll end up being a banker of sorts, shipping games as early as April and May but not receiving any payment until October. The real kicker here is that if your game takes off, you'll receive several large reorders that will have to be financed before the giant chains will even think about sending you payment for the first shipment.

The buyers for these chains are bombarded daily by every toy and game entrepreneur in existence. Substantial evidence will be required to convince these folks to take a gamble on your product. It won't be all that difficult to get an appointment with them, but you're likely to find yourself up against a polite stone wall unless your game and/or promotion is red hot.

2. Educational Market. Includes retail, wholesale, public and private schools and libraries that sell or use items intended for education either in a school setting or at home.

While many pre-school and early school games cross over into the type of market described above, there is a surprising number aimed directly at educators and institutions. This market can't approach the potential sales of the traditional market, but it can be a good starting point for a new game. There are wholesalers and retailers serving this market specifically, as well as some fairly big direct mail catalogue operations. In addition, there's the more obvious route of selling to educators and institutions via telemarketing and state and national shows and conferences. The key to this market will be your ability to demonstrate the tangible educational value of your product, and the method for using it in a classroom setting.

3. Book Market. Includes retail and wholesale operations, as well as public and private libraries, that sell or lend various items, but primarily books.

This market is larger than the toy/game market in that more money is spent on books in this country than on toys and games. There are more book retailers because of this, and if a game fits into a major book merchandiser's plans, it may do decent volume off of one or two accounts. Not every game, however, is suitable for this market. The ones that have done well in the past have had some kind of tie-in with popular books. For example, TRIVIAL PURSUIT did well in the book market long before it became a mass merchandised item, because buyers saw that trivia books had done well for a number of years. Word games are always hopeful entries into the book market because of their natural connection.

Since the success of TRIVIAL PURSUIT and other games like it in this market, buyers seem a little less resistant to opening small game sections in their stores. They can't carry the more common popular games so they must consider lesser known items - which creates an opportunity for quality products with the appropriate subject-matter.

Comprised of retail and wholesale operations engaged in marketing gift items in general, and the Stationery Market. For all practical purposes this category will be treated the same as the gift market except that there are often separate trade shows for stationery items. In addition, many department store chains sell adult, high-priced games in their stationery sections.

4. The Gift Market.   According to past marketing surveys, half the games purchased in the U.S. are bought as gifts. Obviously they're not all bought in gift stores per se, but this market shouldn't be overlooked. There are over 60,000 gift shops in the country, so if a game finds a niche in this area it has a good chance of being around for a while.

5. The Stationery Market.   On the other side of the coin there's the stationery departments, mostly found in retail chains. They tend to have a select few games not normally available through mass merchandisers. While these outlets can't sell millions of games, they do quite well and tend to be more open to trying new products. One big disadvantage is that they tend to drop games as the novelty wears off, so be prepared to see a huge slump in sales after the second year of dealing with these people if you haven't developed other markets. While it may be easier to enter this market than others, it still isn't a cinch. You must have a first class product: it can stand to be a little pricey, but it must be top quality.

6. Specialty Market.   A market or industry not normally exposed to games, but for reasons of subject matter can offer a potential market to a particular game.

Here's where a game can really shine. This is a market uncluttered by other games and one that will accept a higher retail price tag. Sound like a perfect place for what you've got? Let's see!

Recently I was involved in producing a game based on leasing land and drilling for oil. It was a beautiful game with a large number of quality components and excellent play value. It was also expensive to produce and currently has a suggested retail value of $30, a bit high for the traditional board game market. The inventor decided not to go after traditional markets, but concentrated instead on a few retail outlets and a handful of the most exclusive stores in the country. The main market he targeted was one where there was no competition at all - the oil and gas industry. Most of the marketing was directed toward large firms with healthy profit margins who could afford to buy up to a thousand of these items to give away as gifts to clients and prospective customers. Instead of settling for the $12 to $15 they'd get from a distributor, the game's producers pulled in between $20 and $24 a unit. They plan to edge slowly into the mass market, after demand has already been established.

Another example of specialty games involves one that is currently coming out of the planning stages and getting ready for production. It's a real estate development game which the owners intend to market in a similar manner to the oil game. Virtually all their efforts will go into direct mail and telemarketing aimed at commercial real estate brokers and developers, construction companies, city planners and architectural firms. In addition, they plan to attend trade shows. This game also carries a suggested retail price of $30 and is being pushed as a unique, novel gift item. A third game currently in the works is intended for the medical industry; it will retail for a whopping $50 to $60.

One feature all these games have in common is very high quality and a sophisticated look. No corners have been cut to save production costs, which means the negative side of this approach is cost. The games are expensive to produce, but because of the market can demand a high price tag. When considering this market, determine how much you can afford to spend to obtain a quality look.

THE PSYCHOLOGY OF BUYING

Before delving into a discussion of the four sub-markets, it's a good idea to consider what they have in common - and that is the buyers. If the old adage, "Nothing happens until somebody sells something", is true then it follows that there's no sale until somebody buys something. And therein lies the rub. Buyers are not a stagnant bunch. They are usually on their way up, down or out. Nobody but a masochist would want to be a buyer. They are under constant pressure to produce while computers keep an eye on their progress. The more important the store they work for, the more demand is placed on their time by every individual and firm with an item to sell. With IBM's coldly calculating the results of their decisions, once buyers establish a successful department, it can be easier to move a mountain than to get them to make a change.

When a salesperson pushing a new item sits down with a buyer, he is essentially asking the buyer to do a lot more than just try his product. Every department or section of a store is expected to generate a profit, which is usually based on the square footage of the area. For the department to generate its required profit quota, each item in it must meet certain minimums. If one item falls, it brings down the overall profits and is replaced. Through a process of experience, knowledge, instinct and sweat each buyer strives to create a department that at the very least meets the minimum.

**Convincing the Buyer
to Try Your Game**

Enter the unknown: a new salesperson with a new item put out by a new company. It's enough to terrify any self-respecting buyer who's sweated blood to establish better-than-average profits. Now there's this person trying to convince him to replace an item that is at least meeting minimum requirements, with a product that has virtually no track record in sales. Furthermore, the new item may or may not be made by a company that will be able to meet higher demands should sales zoom. No thank you, sir. Get the picture? You'd better be able to convince the buyer that your game will do better than the worst selling one on his shelf.

A second, though perhaps minor objection often raised by store buyers, is the fact that they can't buy from you until you have been registered as an authorized vendor for their firm. To register a company requires between $2000 and $4000 worth of man hours and computer time, in the case of the big chain stores. The buyer won't get excited about having all this expense attributed to his department for a single item that might not even sell. You'll hear a lot of objections to one-item lines for this reason, in addition to the endless task of simply handling the order. There's no pat answer to this objection but it is heartening to note that PENTE, UNO and even TRIVIAL PURSUIT were once one-item lines. The problem is not insurmountable, but you're going to have to work hard to persuade the buyer that your product is well worth the extra effort.

The best advice I can offer in dealing with game buyers is to be patient, honest and sincere. They don't like to say 'no' but their job demands it a good deal of the time, so you're best not trying to push them into a corner. You have to ask for the order - that's your job - but their job is to say 'yes' or 'no'. If you force a decision, you may just be forcing a 'no'. Now on to the prospect of selling to the major markets through their sub-markets.

THE SUB-MARKETS Direct mail has some distinct advantages and disadvantages over the other marketing strategies. A major advantage is that it brings in the full retail price - there are no discounts involved - in addition to the two or three dollars charged for postage and handling. Just for fun let's go back to the hypothetical print run of 2500 games that cost $7.88 apiece. Assuming we managed to sell them all through direct mail at the full retail price of $16, we'll gross sales of $40,000 less COG of $19,700. This means a net profit of $20,300, or a 103% return on the original investment before deducting our cost of sales. Realistically, this isn't likely to happen, but you get the point. Direct mail sales, no matter the volume, can generate a high profit margin and a positive cash flow (which means that more money is coming in than going out). The other advantage of direct mail sales is the effect they have on word-of-mouth advertising. People who buy games through the mail tend to play those games and tell others about them.

Cost of Advertising The downside to this method is the cost of advertising. Ads have to appear constantly in magazines where potential customers are likely to see them. I've been told an ad needs to appear three times consecutively in order to be effective. It's better, too, if all three ads are different, as people tend to pass over advertisements they've already read. In addition, you should realize that ads don't necessarily pay for themselves right away. People tend to put magazines aside for a while, picking them up again at a later date. What this means is that you'll be paying for the ads over a period of time. True, there's a price break for frequency but the ads had better pull enough sales to cover expenses.

Order Processing A second disadvantage to direct sales is the processing of orders. When selling one game at a time, orders have to be filled one game at a time. Each item must be packaged, addressed, recorded, and then shipped. If mail order sales are strong and steady, consider hiring a young person to work after school. Better yet, draft one of your own children. It probably is about time they started to earn their keep. In any event, processing those one game orders, regardless of how happy you are to get them, can become a tedious task.

Be sure to get corrugated wrappers to protect your games in shipping. These usually can be obtained from companies who maintain stocks of standard size boxes; or you can have them custom made.

If your mail order business volume is not great, you probably are better off buying a few at a time from someone who stocks them, even though they may not be an exact fit. If a hundred or more games a week are being shipped on a direct mail basis, it may be wise to have some custom made. If so, don't have cartons made; wrappers are cheaper and do just as well. Tell the box maker you want the kind of wrapper used to ship books. He'll know what you are talking about.

Direct Mail Sales   Before going on to another market, let's reexamine some of the ways direct mail sales can be obtained. The most common method is through magazine ads. These can be extremely costly if the ad doesn't work well. Do some research, on both the magazines and the other direct mail ads which reappear in them. Find out about the readers. In some cases it may be necessary to design a special ad for a magazine. When using this approach make sure to 'key' the ads. Keying ads means adding a code to the address; that will tell you the orders came from a specific ad in a specific magazine. Keep records of the results. They will show where advertising money is working and where it isn't. After sixty to ninety days of running ads and evaluating results, you may decide to run a larger ad in a magazine which pulled well, and/or drop an ad from one that didn't. Continuing to run an advertisement in a magazine which is not pulling in orders is just throwing good money after bad. Pay attention to this area. You will learn soon how to get the most out of your mail order advertising investment.

Sales Through Retail   The next market area is retail outlets, almost all independents (non-
Outlets   chain), and mostly the mom and pop operations touched on earlier. There are literally thousands of these stores and they should become an excellent source of sales. They are actually easier to reach than consumers but more difficult to sell. They offer their own advantages and disadvantages.

The least expensive way to reach these retailers is go to the yellow pages, find a firm which supplies mailing lists, and call them up Ask if they have a list of X number of a certain type of store. They will check, call back, and tell you what is available and how much it is going to cost. Then you have a mailing piece printed and give it to the mailing house to send to your newly-acquired list. It's the least expensive method I know to reach large numbers of prospective buyers in a highly concentrated market. When buying the list, ask if it's possible to obtain a computer printout of the names and addresses with phone numbers. If a list with phone numbers is not available, try to get a list without numbers and go to the library to look them up. The reason for this is – you guessed it – you are going to ease into telemarketing.

Back to your mailing program for a moment ...It really won't hurt to mail your piece 'Bulk Rate'. It's the lowest postage cost. Each mailer takes a little longer to get where it's going, but it usually gets there. What is really important, whether it's mailed bulk rate, first class, registered, or certified, is the piece itself. It has to be eye catching, interesting, appealing, unusual, and brief. If it isn't, guess where it is going ten seconds after its opened. Right, the old circular file, more commonly known as the waste basket.

Promoting to the Retailers

The flyer has to make an impression. You hope it will inspire at least a few mail or phone orders. But even if it doesn't, it still needs to make an impression so these merchants will remember the product when they are called or mailed to again.

When designing the flyer, feel free to "borrow" from the magazine ads you have seen and liked. On this first mailing piece especially, a good, picture of the game is essential, and the picture must be large enough to be easily identifiable. Another essential is heavy bold type announcing discount available to the retailers.

Most stores buy staple items through distributors, at least when distributors stock them. In this case, there won't be any distributors to begin with, so make the retailers aware – in both the flyer and follow-up phone calls – that the item is not yet available through normal distribution channels. At this point you are selling direct to stores.

Selling Through Distributors

When a retailer buys from a distributor his discount usually is forty percent off the retail price. If an item has a suggested retail price of ten dollars, the retailer pays the distributor six. This discount applies to the toy industry. In the gift market, a large market section which has surprisingly few major distributors, the discount offered the retailer is approximately fifty percent off the suggested retail. One thing which works well is to offer an additional discount for prompt payment. Normal terms in both the toy and gift markets state that invoices are payable thirty days after receipt of goods. To help create positive cash flow and keep accountants and creditors happy, try offering these terms: 40% net thirty; 10% net ten days. What all this means is the dealer earns the forty percent discount if he pays the invoice within thirty days of receiving the merchandise and an additional ten percent if he pays within ten days. That's not ten percent off the top. If you are not familiar with discount structures, now is the time to become so. Here's an example that should help.

A game retails for $10.00. A store buys 100 copies, for a total retail value of one thousand dollars. The store's discount is forty percent, net thirty days, which means it owes six hundred dollars if payment is made within thirty days.

If the retailer is really managing his business (and enjoys a positive cash flow), he pays within ten days to get the extra ten percent discount. Then he only pays five hundred and forty dollars. To show how it all works out, look at the following arithmetic:

Retail value equals	$1,000.00
40% discount	$400.00
Net due in thirty days	$600.00
10% prompt payment discount	$60.00
Net due in ten days	$540.00

It really is simple. Whenever a string of discounts appear,the first applies to the retail value; then the rest apply in sequence against the preceding net amount.

Mom and Pop Retail Operations

Mom and Pop type operations can be very good business for game sales ... sometimes. Other times they can be more trouble than they are worth. By and large the owners and operators of these stores are hard working folks who pay attention to their local market and know almost instinctively what will and what won't in their stores. No matter how positive they 'feel' about a new product, especially one not from a major manufacturer with strong advertising support, they are likely to be skeptical and cautious at first. They probably will want to order six or less of the item to see how it does. Some may even try to buy on consignment. Initially these small quantities – even the consignment orders – will be all right, assuming the buyers are paying the shipping charges, because of a point of view which typically exists in small stores.

Don't Oversell!   If three copies of a game go to a store and are all sold within two weeks, the retailer notices, to his pleasant surprise, that he is sold out. It creates a re-ordering frame of mind. But if six copies are sold to the same store and if three of them are left at the end of the same two week period, the frame of mind created is negative. The merchant thinks he bought too many and the item is not moving well. The moral, of course, is don't oversell these people. It's far better, in the long run, to let them order small quantities at first. If the game starts to do well, and they continue to run out and reorder, they will have nothing but praise for the product. That attitude will become a significant factor in further increasing sales. It may not seem important, but in an independent retail operation, the owner's and employees' attitude about a product is everything. These are not huge, impersonal discount houses. These are small shops with a lot of repeat customers. The people who work there can only compete with the mass merchandisers by offering service. The service they offer is, more often then not, courtesy and in-depth knowledge of the products on their shelves. When a customer asks, "What's a good game to buy", you want them to say," This one is really doing well. Why not try it?"

So, a modest sales approach is right for this market. Even if you have a friend who owns a store, resist the urge to take advantage of that relationship by selling him three hundred copies of the game at one time. It won't help either one of you.

Overcoming the skepticism and caution of these buyers is going to require determination. It will be necessary to contact them repeatedly by mail or phone, as well as in person whenever possible. Send the same piece two or three times. Send post cards. In fact a post card can be an effective and inexpensive method of mailing follow ups.

A Telephone Sales Approach That Worked   One lady I know of had a full color picture of her game printed on card stock and cut into postcards. She mailed a normal eight and one-half by eleven inch advertisement initially then began making her follow-up calls. As she made each call, she kept a customer card for each shop, filling it in with as much information as she could gather, including the names of the owners and, more importantly, the person who ordered games, and just about anything else that was passed on in conversation. These people, once they open up, love to talk about their stores and their knowledge of the industry, but getting them to open up is difficult. The lady would try to chat with each store she called, introducing herself and her product as a first effort. She made no bones about letting them know she wanted them to buy her game, but she didn't push it too hard. When they started to make some excuse to get off the phone she would change the subject by asking what games sold best in their store, or what kind of people frequented their shop – anything to keep the person talking. As the merchant spoke, she made notes on a sheet of scratch paper while watching a clock. When the timer was approaching three minutes she would politely bring the conversation to a close by telling the person several things. She told them she had to get off the phone before the long distance charges bankrupted her. She genuinely appreciated their time and would like to call them again to ask their opinion (people do love to give opinions) about the best way to go about marketing her item. Then she asked if it would be all right if she called them back on a certain day about a month away. When they had agreed to a date, she would thank them again for their time and say something like, " Well, it's really been pleasant speaking with you. You have been very helpful. You must really know this business. I'm looking forward to talking to you again, when I can afford it. When I call we'll write an order, OK?"

Now this may seem very innocent, but believe me it's not. In fact this woman was the most deadly phone sales person I've ever run across. The number of orders she took on her second or third call was phenomenal. The reason for this success – her manner and tactics.

Her first call was very casual, not pushy at all, though she did tell them very quickly she had called to sell games. After that she let it rest, drawing them out with questions about a subject they could speak on knowledgeably and with confidence. The more the other person spoke, the more confident they became and the less intimidated they were by talking to a 'salesperson'. When she closed the conversation she made them aware she was not rich. Most of them aren't either and were able to identify with that. Then she made an appointment to call again, creating a certain feeling of obligation on the part of the person to whom she was speaking. At the very end she announces that she will ask for an order from them and asked if this would be 'OK'. This sets the person up to give her an order on the next call. Even if the person is not consciously aware he or she is committing to place an order when they next speak, the suggestion has been planted.

After the call is over, the lady fills out her customer card with the information she has obtained. Then, before preparing to call the next number, she writes out a post card saying something relevant and personal, confirming the date of her next call. The card is then put into a date folder and mailed two weeks from the day.

No one can guarantee the results of any system, but of all the results I've seen from people entering the game market for the first time, this approach has to be the most effective. True, it requires time and money; but about the third time you call these people you could be closing (getting orders) as many as fifteen percent. As these shops become your customers, calls become more productive. You can stop mailing every month and concentrate on opening new markets. But before going on to some of those new markets, let's look at some basic rules for making telephone sales.

Always Ask for the Order   The golden rule is ASK FOR AN ORDER! No matter how indirect or easy your manner, not asking is wasting time and money. When I train someone to work the phones I make it a point to get them to ask for the order at least three times during the conversation. I want them to be polite, and not overly pushy, but if they don't ask, it's not very likely they will make a sale. Some ways of asking politely could be," could I get you to try...", "Could you test my product by taking...", or, in a half joking manner preceded by a chuckle," What am I going to have to do to get you to give this a try?" You'll come up with your own style to suit your personality. But remember, if you're not going to ask, don't bother to call.

The second rule of telemarketing is STAY ON THE PHONE. You are playing a numbers game. If you don't believe playing the odds really works, check out the insurance industry. Their whole business is based on statistics. They have, are, and always will make fortunes. There is an interesting story I once heard about a real estate agent who was using telemarketing to sell land in Hawaii. It's worth repeating because it clicks perfectly with all types of telephone sales.

This industrious, determined fellow created a list of around fifty thousand island residents who were likely prospects. He set up a telephone marketing room, hired and trained people to man the phones, and then dove right in. Each month, every person on the list was contacted regarding a specific real estate investment offer.

Telemarketing – It takes Persistence

After a few months, many of the people were getting down- right rude, telling the callers never to bother them again. Undaunted, the callers kept calling ... every month. At first it seemed the operation was destined to fail. There were some sales, but they fell far short of expectations. Then things began to turn around. About a year into the operation an analysis of the records revealed some interesting things.

Some of the people who had been rude and insisted on not being called again had invested. After the first investments, people tended to become more or less regular clients. But the most amazing statistic retrieved was the fact that eighty percent of the people investing for the first time did so after the fifth contact.

Interestingly enough, our own telemarketing program selling games to retail outlets produced almost identical results. In addition, several other telemarketing studies offer similar statistics to back up the findings. The lesson is fairly obvious; persistence pays off.

On days when you are working at telemarketing, try to make at least fifty contacts a day. As soon as each call is finished make an accurate record of what was said or arranged. This record keeping can be best done using a card system, which is filed by date. This allows you to see easily when people are to be called back.

Telemarketing is just like any other form of sales. If insults, rudeness, and people saying,'No', are going to cause a loss of faith in yourself or product, you'll be better off dropping the project before it costs a fortune; or at least make arrangements to have someone else do the selling.

Everyone is a little nervous when calling someone they don't know. It's natural, but try to put things in perspective. You're not making first contact with an alien race, you are calling another human, one probably just as nervous as you are. When working on the phone, try to stay as relaxed as possible. Smile, even though nobody can see – it sets a frame of mind and mood. Talk as though you already know the person; after all, if it's a call back – you do.

There are many good telemarketing books available. They contain a tremendous amount of information. If telemarketing is part of the plan, get them and use them.

Importance of Follow-up

Two more things. The first is to follow up the call with a mailing. Whether it's simply a post card confirming your next appointment or a brochure or copies of some press coverage of the game, it's very important to reinforce the personal relationship established with the call.

The last rule of telemarketing is the first rule; ask for the order. It doesn't matter how indirectly, but work it in to the conversation at least three times. You will be amazed at how many people will relent the third time and try your product.

DISTRIBUTORS AND CHAIN STORES

The next market areas to think about are game distributors and chain stores. Though they share some similarities, the buying habits of both differ from those of a single retail outlet.

Distributors tend to buy larger quantities, but they demand better discounts. A distributor may not buy at all unless the terms are at least 50/10 with freight paid and invoice coming due on the tenth of the month, thirty days after receipt of goods. Remember, that's fifty percent off the retail, then ten percent off the remaining fifty per cent. In this case the ten percent is not for prompt payment: it may be necessary to throw in another five or ten percent to cover this area.

If a distributor has any faith at all in an item he usually will order a gross (twelve dozen). However, they tend to be cautious when ordering a new, unknown item and may start with as few as twenty-four or thirty-six, depending upon their size. A distributor who deals with volume may not order at all until he becomes convinced he'll be able to move at least a gross; otherwise it just isn't worth the paperwork involved in adding a new item to inventory.

Chain Store Buying

Chain stores tend to order quantities based on placing so many of an item in each store. This can vary from as few as six to as many as a gross, depending upon the chain's traffic pattern and volume history. In this case it may be necessary to 'drop-ship'; i.e., split the order and ship to the various locations. Some chains rely on distributors when trying something new. Others will take six for each of a few stores to test market the item. In any event, if a large chain picks up a new item and does well with it, it can become very lucrative even though each store isn't taking a lot individually. For instance, if a chain with three hundred stores is taking six copies of a game for each store every month a quick calculation shows 1800 games per month. That's a whopping 20,600 games a year – from one customer!

But before you start opening the champagne, bear firmly in mind the fact that it's not all that easy to get these people to even try a new product. Most keep a close watch on the market. If a game is selling they know about it by keeping a 'manager's want list'. Since most chains are fairly strict about what goes in their stores they don't allow individual managers much leeway to add something which is not being ordered by their central purchasing department. They do however ask each manager to keep a list of items customers are asking for but are not in stock. If a particular item appears several times on numerous manager's lists, the central buyers will begin investigating the item.

Chain Store Discounts

Discounts for chain stores may have very similar bottom lines to those for distributors – but getting to the bottom line is often by a different route. For example, the discount will probably start at fifty/ten percent off retail. Another five to ten percent may be included as an advertising allowance for the chain, and an additional five may be given for special placement of the game (i.e. an end of the aisle – called an end cap – or window display).Finally, most will ask for two percent if payment is made within thirty days of the due date. So what you might wind up with is a discount which looks something like this: 50/10/5/5/2.

If you are fortunate enough to sell to one of the really large retail chains, don't be surprised to find you suddenly have become a banker as well as a game entrepreneur. In addition to the string of negotiated discounts the chains want something else, something just as important as money – time.

Order Dating   One of the terms with which you'll become familiar in the toy business is "dating". No, you're not about to be taken to dinner and romanced. In the toy industry, as well as in several others, dating terms are applied when a retailer/wholesaler buys a product and has it shipped in the spring, with the first payment due far into the future. For example, in the toy industry, the normal dating payment dates are October 10, December 10 and January 10.

What this means to a small game company is that games will be shipped in March or April to a retailer's units with first payment due on October 10. If the game does well the retailer may reorder in May or June with a new payment date of December 10. Another reorder comes in for September with a January 10 payment date. If it's a big chain and the game's doing well, the game company could have shipped tens of thousands of copies over a seven to eight month period and not have been paid a dime.

As if dating wasn't bad enough, 'anticipation' will cause ulcers among the few game companies that stayed around to try and lasso one of these major chains. Anticipation happens when the chain realizes they are buying lots of games from a company and will be reordering according to a previously negotiated dating program. The chain will pay early – that's the good news, The bad news is they will want an additional discount. Let's say the chain took a ten thousand dollar order in March with October 10 dating. For whatever reasons they decide to pay the bill four months early, say June. On the day they cut the check, they'll document the prime annual interest rate, divide by twelve to come up with an equivalent monthly rate then multiply by the number of months early they're paying. The result is a percentage of the bill which gets deducted before the check is mailed to the manufacturer. For example: the chain owes ten thousand dollars which is due on October tenth; the annual interest rate is twelve percent and the chain is paying four months early. twelve percent divided by twelve months is one percent per month multiplied by four months equals four percent of ten thousand dollars or four hundred dollars which is deducted from the bill.

Unless the distributor or chain store is a very specialized operation it is very difficult to get these people to place a first order. Calling them till you're blue in the face may help but in many cases they prefer to see samples, know exactly where the item is being advertised and how often, who else is carrying the item and, 'Who's your rep?'

Using Manufacturers' Reps

Obviously the companies that buy large volume are constantly bombarded by everybody with anything to sell. They simply don't have time to deal with all these new items. Consequently, a system has developed using manufacturers representatives, or reps. A rep is an independent agent who represents your game or line of products as well as the products of several other companies. The rep's job is to act as sales liaison between manufacturers and high volume buyers. However, just because reps have the ability to show your item to a buyer doesn't mean they will.

A rep has to be discriminating. He walks a razor's edge. If he sells something he knows is wrong for a buyer, he may be out a customer which means he's not only lost future commissions on your item, he's lost them on the other dozen lines of product he offers. On the other hand, if the rep doesn't show and sell a manufacturer's item to enough buyers he's going to be fired and lose the line.

Many reps are simply not interested in trying to sell a one item line. They feel it's not worth their effort to try to carve out a niche in the market place for a single game. When a rep takes a line, he obtains perpetuity for a particular territory. If the rep's territory is the midwest, then the rep gets paid his ten to fifteen percent commission on every item sold in any of his states - regardless of who actually sells them. Like every other profession there are good reps and there are bad reps. If you get a bad one, watch out - he'll cost more money than he makes.

One rule of thumb is to watch the orders the rep places in the first ninety days of selling. Don't pay any attention to what he says about 'the big one he's about to close'. If he or she is not writing a lot more orders with new customers than were being written before a rep covered the area, fire 'em. Don't be afraid to hurt their feelings, A bad rep gets fired all the time but hardly anybody fires a good one.

Do Your Own Marketing First

Its a good idea to try to sell this market yourself at first. When things start developing, reps will seek you out and you'll be able to pick and choose for each territory. When reps do begin calling ask them for the names and numbers of other manufacturers they represent. If you've never heard of the companies the rep is either not a particularly great one or just getting started with his firm. If the companies are known, give them a call, ask to speak with the sales manager and question the rep's record. How long has he been their rep? Has he increased sales? By what percentage? How much new business? This approach not only will save you a lot of grief in the long run, it may even help find a rep who will give your sales a real boost.

But no matter what, never take a pig in a poke. No rep is better than a bad one!

Distributors and chain stores should and can become the biggest market for a game. But at first, until the game has generated genuine demand in the marketplace, concentrate on direct mail, retail outlets and, if there is one, a specialty market.

COPYRIGHTS, PATENTS AND TRADEMARKS

Since I am not an attorney and do not carry the necessary insurance to speak freely on the subject of legal protection, (and since I am both lazy and wise enough to let someone else do the work for me if possible) and since this book desperately needs a section on this subject, I have procured the required information from a friend named Tom Timmons. Tom is a founding partner of Kanz, Scherback & Timmons, a Dallasbased law firm specializing in, among other things, trademarks, patents and copyrights.

In today's legalistic world it's virtually impossible to stay successful without the services of at least one good lawyer. Picking one to contribute to this work reminded me of my favorite attorney story.

It seems a very wealthy industrialist called his three most trusted associates and friends – his accountant, priest and attorney – to his death bed. Looking pale and weak, he handed each of them a thick, sealed envelope and said, "I've always disliked the old saying, 'you can't take it with you', and I've figured away to beat it. Each of those envelopes contains 100 thousand dollars in cash. After I have been lowered into the grave and everyone else has left, I want you three to toss those envelopes into the grave then stay until the hole is filled."

The three men looked at each other strangely but tucked the envelopes away and left. A few weeks later, at their friend's funeral they followed his last wishes, throwing the envelopes in and watching the workers fill the hole. As the sun was going down they sat silently in the back seat of a limousine headed toward town.

Halfway there the accountant turns to the priest and says, "Father, I must confess, I couldn't stand watching the money be thrown away. There were only 60 thousand dollars in my envelope."

"Glory Be", says the priest, greatly relieved,"I must confess meself, I couldn't stand the thought of all that money going to waste and I took fifty thousand out for the poor box."

"I am appalled. I am shocked!", said the lawyer, "We were his best friends, his most trusted associates. It was his dying request, for God's sake. I just want the record to show that in my envelope there was my personal check for one hundred thousand dollars."

The point of the story is some lawyers exist solely to make a damn fine living in the legal jungle they have grown around us, others are there to make a fine living as well as to help a few people in the process. Tom is one who has always been there to help when I needed advice.

* * * * * * *

PROTECTING YOUR GAME

One of the worst shocks a game inventor can experience is to discover he or she has accidentally dedicated it to the public or unintentionally shared whatever rights exist with a commercial artist. These problems can be avoided and certain protections can be built into the game as it is developed. Ideally, you would like to protect the concept of the game itself, the main idea. You also want to protect the appearance of the game, the artwork which appears on the box, board, rules, cards or any other materials used with the game. Along with the artwork, you would like to protect whatever words are used for the game, including the way the rules are expressed in addition to any writing appearing on the gameboard or playing cards. Finally, in order to eventually have valuable trademark rights, you must use a trademark correctly from the beginning. Probably the simplest guide to obtain these different kinds of protection is simply to purchase a similar type of game which is produced by a major manufacturer. Study the way that manufacturer protects its own game, and that can provide a guide for your own use. We can begin by picking up a SCRABBLE crossword game manufactured by Selchow & Righter Co..

Protecting the Concept – Patents and Trade Secrets

There are only two ways of protecting a concept, through patents and trade secrets. As you open the SCRABBLE box and lay open the board, notice the notation "Patent No. 2,752,158." It's known as a "patent notice" and it serves to notify people the game is patented, (or rather it was patented since that patent expired many years ago). A patent is nearly an ideal form of protection since it does protect the general concept, at least to the extent that the concept meets the requirements of being patentable. In order to be a patentable invention, an item must be new, useful, and unobvious. The general concept of a board game is, of course, not new and neither is the idea of a board game with tiles or cards or dice. It is, however, possible to have a board game made up of those elements which is new in the way it combines those elements.

Patents have several problems, not the least of which is they are expensive and difficult to obtain. Plan on spending a minimum of 4,000 dollars before obtaining a patent on even a fairly simple concept. Also plan on a minimum of 12-15 months from the time the application is first filed before it issues. Finally, patent applications undergo a tough examination and are frequently rejected.

One final word about patents is worthwhile since there is such widespread misunderstanding concerning them. Patents are not self-enforcing. The government does not enforce a patent except occasionally in the case of infringing imports, so you must be prepared to go to court to enforce your patent. The good news is patents are usually respected; and even in a situation where there is infringement, it normally can be stopped without having to go to court. Infringers have to worry about court costs and attorneys fees as much as patent owners, but they have the additional worry of possible damage payments to the patent owner.

Confidentiality Agreements

There is one other way of protecting a concept, through trade secrets. While a game is being developed it can be kept secret. In order to keep it a secret, it is necessary to have confidentiality agreements with everyone who is told about the game. This includes printers, artists and even potential investors. The confidentiality agreements need to describe the game in sufficient detail to identify it, but not in such detail as to give away any secret information in the agreement itself. It can be quite a trick but it can be done.

Artwork and Writings – Copyrights

Look on the inside of the SCRABBLE box lid where the rules of play are printed. At the bottom of the rules is the copyright notice,"Copyright 1948, 1949, 1953 by Selchow & Righter Co." The three years listed mean the words used to describe the rules for playing were first published in 1948 and they were then changed sufficiently in 1949 and 1953 to justify registering copyrights for the new editions. The copyright does not protect the general concept, but it does protect the way the rules are expressed. Whereas, a patent only lasts for 17 years from the date it issues, copyrights last for 75 years from the date of first publication for corporate authors and run years past the death of the last joint author for individuals. Now look at the gameboard again, on the lower right hand corner there's another copyright notice, "Copyright 1948 by Selchow & Righter Co." This one copyrights the artwork on the game board. If the SCRABBLE crossword game had artwork on the box it would also be copyrighted and bear its own copyright notice.

There are two aspects to copyright. One is the copyright notice which includes either the word "Copyright" or "Copr." or the letter "C" written in a circle along with the year the particular copyrighted word, the particular board or set of rules, is first made available to the public and the name of the copyright owner. The copyright notice must appear on every copy of the game. If a game does not show the copyright notice, there is a danger of dedicating your artwork and words to the public.

The second aspect to remember about the copyright is the registration. The registration is a formality but should be done as soon as possible. It is not necessary to obtain the registration or even to file it before publication or printing the notice. Registrations are relatively inexpensive, normally running no more than a couple of hundred dollars even through an attorney.

Protecting Trademarks

Examine the lid of the SCRABBLE box. The trademark SCRABBLE appears on the top of the box and on all four edges in bold capital letters. In all five places, the description term "crossword game" appears written below the trademark in much smaller letters. In every case, the letter "R" is written in a small circle to the upper right of the trademark. The circled "R" is proper notice the trademark SCRABBLE is registered with the U.S. Patent and Trademark Office.

You are not permitted to even apply for federal registration unless the game is actually being sold in at least two states or in international commerce. Once the federal registration is applied for it could easily be a year or more before the registration is granted. What you are allowed to use is the combination of the letters "TM" which tells the world "this is my trademark and not a generic term." You do not need a registration in order to use the TM. Even without a registration, the rights obtained strictly from usage can still be valuable and enforceable.

The SCRABBLE trademark also appears on the insides of the cover at the beginning of the rules as well as on all four edges of the game board. In total, the trademark appears on the box and board 11 times. In every case, the trademark is in large bold letters. Every time it appears on the outside of the box, it is accompanied by the descriptive term "crossword game" as well as the trademark registration notice. This is good trademark usage and a good model to follow.

Computer Games

Computer games differ from board games in that they also have computer software which can be copyrighted. Once again, it is a good idea to take an established company's product as a model. The INFOCOM games are especially creative in the way they call a user's attention to the copyright notice which appears on the screen. IN addition, you will find a copyright notice in the written material and on the diskette label. The INFOCOM games also illustrate a different example of trademark usage. The trademark INFOCOM is the "house mark" for a series of computer games. Each computer game within the series also bears its own trademark such as SORCERER or ENCHANTER. The use of both trademarks on the same game is not inconsistent since one represents the entire line and the other represents the particular product.

Finally, one special caution needs to be made with regard to copyrights. Pretend for a moment you have just developed an extraordinary computer game, but you need help in writing the computer software. You engage an independent contractor to write the program for you, but have no written agreement or one which makes no mention of copyright ownership. The independent contractor develops the software according to specifications and delivers it. You hand the contractor a check for the agreed amount. The independent contractor thanks you for the check and on his way out mentions,"I hope you like the software which I developed for you. By the way, let me know if you would also like the right to sell it to other people." You know it has not been a good day. The same thing can happen when an independent artist develops the artwork for your game! You need written agreement with all independent contractors, and the written agreements need to specify that the independent contractor will assign all copyrights to you.

* * * * *

It may be possible to file for some of the registrations yourself but I don't recommend it. As I said before, it's a crazy world; a brewery in Colorado can get sued over a drunk driving accident in California because the driver drank their beer. Get a lawyer; you'll sleep better and so will I.

APPENDIX

TRADE SHOWS AND CONVENTIONS

The following is a list of trade shows and conventions which may may be helpful in bringing a game to market. Each industry usually will have its own trade shows and if a game legitimately bridges two or more industries it may be a good idea to attend shows in all of those industries. On the other hand, if the game really doesn't cross over it probably is a waste of time and money to try and force it in a market where it doesn't belong. For instance, the people with the game about building houses may do well attending trade shows in the toy and building/construction industries but would likely do miserably at a book show.

More shows exist than are listed here. The reasons are simple. First, no one needs to or can attend every show which takes place. In fact, it's physically impossible for one person to even work every day at every show in just the gift industry. Only major shows in each industry are listed. Second, many shows are not long lived. If not established, they may draw large crowds for a year or two then, as attendance drops, vanish from the circuit.

Toy Shows – Trade

Trade shows for the toy industry are listed below. These shows generally are not open to the public and exhibit space must be booked a considerable time in advance. The name of the show is followed by the month in which it is held, the location, who to contact for more information (a phone number or address) and, occasionally, notes on the show.

International Toy Fair – January
Paris, France
(212) 869- 1720

Harrogate International Toy Fair – January
North Yorkshire, England
(212) 752-8400

Hobby Industry of America Convention – January
Location varies.
(201) 794-1133

Only certain types of games tend to do well at this show so get a copy of last year's attendance list and check to see the types of games being sold there.

Milan Toy Fair – January
Milan, Italy
E-A Salone

International Fair
Del Giocattolo via petit
Milan, Italy

British Toy and Hobby Fair – January
London, England
(212) 752-8400

Canadian Toy and Decoration Fair – January
Toronto, Canada
(416) 893-1689

Nuremberg Toy Fair – February
Nuremberg, Germany

International Speilwarenmesse
DgMBh 85
Nuremberg, West Germany

American Toy Fair – February
New York City
(212) 675-1141

This is the big one, at least for this country. Very important to have representation at both the permanent show rooms at the 200 Fifth Avenue Building and the temporary exhibitors hall.

Midwest Toy & Hobby Show – March
Chicago, Illinois
(614) 452- 4541

Dallas Toy Show – March
Dallas, Texas
(214) 655-6100

Southeastern Toy Fair – March
Atlanta, Georgia
(404) 231-2320

Western States Toy and Hobby Show – April
Los Angeles, California
(213)380-2229

International Toy Fair – May
Tokyo, Japan

Japan International Toy Fair Association
11-14, 3-Chome
Kotobuki, Taito-Ku, Tokyo, JN

GENCON – August
Lake Geneva, Wisconsin
P.O. Box 756
Lake Geneva, WI 53147

This one is really mostly a consumer convention focusing on fantasy/role playing games but sometimes a good place to show new product to consumers.

Dallas Toy Show – September
Dallas, Texas
(214) 655-6186

Southeastern Spring/Summer Toy Fair – September
Atlanta, Georgia
(404) 231-2320

New England Toy Rep Show – October
Stoughton, Massachusetts
(617) 449-2345

Spring & Summer Toy & Hobby Show – October
Los Angeles, California
(213)380-2229

Hong Kong Toy & Gift Fair – October
Hong Kong
(212) 730-0777

Taiwan Toy & Gift Fair – October
Taipei, Taiwan
(212) 532-7055

Toy Manufacturers of America – December
New York, New York
(212) 675-1141

Gift Shows – Trade   At last count there were 128 different gift shows conducted annually within the United States. If each show averaged three days in length there would be more show days in the year than there are days in the year. The major shows are listed below.

Atlanta National Gift Show – January
Atlanta Market Center
Atlanta, Georgia
(404) 688-8994

The Beckman Gift Show – January
L.A. Sports Arena
Los Angeles, California
(213) 682-3661

L.A. Gift Mart – January
L.A. Mart
Los Angeles, California
(213) 749-7911

Charlotte Mart – January
Charlotte Merchandise Mart
Charlotte, North Carolina
(704) 377-5881

Dallas Gift Show – January
Dallas Market Center
Dallas, Texas
(214) 655-6276

Chicago Mart Gift Show – January
Chicago Mart
Chicago, Illinois
(312) 527-4141

Chicago Gift Show – January
McCormick Place
Chicago, Illinois
(212) 686-6070

San Francisco Gift Show – February
Moscone Center
San Francisco, California
(415) 621-7345

San Francisco Gift Center – February
S.F. Gift Center
San Francisco, California
(415) 861-7733

New York Gift Show – February
Javits Center
New York, New York
(212) 686-6070

New York Merchandise Mart – February
New York, New York
(212) 686-1203

New York Gift Building – February
225 Fifth Avenue
New York, New York
(212) 685-6377

National Stationery Show – May
Javits Center
New York, New York
(212) 686-6070

Dallas Gift Show – July
Dallas Market Center
Dallas, Texas
(214) 655-6276

Atlanta National Gift Show – July
Atlanta Market Center
Atlanta, Georgia
(404) 688-8994

The Beckman Gift Show – July
L.A. Sports Arena
Los Angeles, California
(213) 665-5713

L.A. Mart – July
L.A. Mart
Los Angeles, California
(213) 749-7911

California Gift Show – July
Convention Center
Los Angeles, California
(213) 682-3661

Chicago Mart Gift Show – July
Chicago Mart
Chicago, Illinois
(312) 527-4141

Chicago Gift Show – July
McCormick Place
Chicago, Illinois
(212) 686-6070

San Francisco Gift Show – August
Moscone Center
San Francisco, California
(415) 621-7345

San Francisco Gift Center – August
S.F. Gift Center
San Francisco, California
(415) 861-7733

New York Gift Show – August
Javits Center
New York, New York
(212) 686-6070

New York Merchandise Mart – August
New York, New York
(212) 686-1203

New York Gift Building – August
225 Fifth Avenue
New York, New York
(212) 685-6377

California Stationery – Show August
San Diego, California
(212) 686-6070

Educational Shows   Each state has one or more conventions for its educators, teachers and administrators. Most of these shows are open to vendors to rent exhibit space. If a game has genuine inherent educational value these shows may prove to be the most effective. There are two major national shows listed below. To find out about individual state shows contact the appropriate state agency.

National Education Association Convention – June or July
Moves from city to city
(202) 833-4000

Educational Dealers & Supply Association Show – March or April
Moves from city to city
(818) 331-7633

Book Shows   There are a number of regional small book shows. The two listed below are the largest and to obtain information on others contact either or both of the associations below.

American Booksellers Association Book Show – April or May
Moves from city to city
(212) 867-9060

American Library Association Convention – May or June
Moves from city to city
(312) 944-6780

TRADE ASSOCIATIONS

The following is a list of associations which are related to the gaming industry. It is not always necessary to join the organizations to obtain help in getting information as most exist to promote their particular industry.

Electronic Industries Association Consumer Electronic Group
2001 Eye Street
Washington, D.C. 20006
202-457-4919

Hobby Industries Of America
319 East 54th Street
Elmwood, NJ 07407
201-794-1133

Juvenile Products Manufacturers Association
66 East Main Street
Moorestown, NJ 08057
609-234-9155

Midwest Toy & Hobby Association
100 East Ogden Avenue
Westmont, IL 60559
312-850-7977

Southwestern Toy & Hobby Association
World Trade Center #58310
Dallas, TX 75258
214-742-2448

Toy Wholesalers' Association of America
66 E. Main Street
Moorestown, NJ 08067
609-234-9155

American Booksellers Association
122 East 42nd Street
New York, NY 10168
212-867-9060

American Library Association
50 East Huron Street
Chicago, IL 60611
312-944-6780

Educational Dealers and Suppliers Association
P.O. Box 3551
Covina, CA 91722
818-331-7633

GLOSSARY OF PRINTING TERMS

Art Director – Individual in charge of one or more artist who directs their efforts.

Artwork – An image prepared for graphic reproduction.

Banding – The wrapping of a package with string, rubber bands, etc., to secure the contents as a single unit.

Basic Weight – The weight of 500 sheets of a particular size and class of paper.

Blueline – Photographic proofs consisting of blue images on white background.

Book – Any published work longer than 64 pages.

Booklet – Any published work of 64 pages or less.

Breaking for Color – Dividing artwork into specific color overlays, or forms, during the artwork stages.

Brownline – A photographic proof consisting of brown images on white background.

Buyouts – Services purchased from an outside source.

C1S – Paper stock which is coated on one side.

C2S – Paper stock which is coated on both sides.

Caliper – see *paper caliper*.

Camera-ready Art – Graphic artwork which is ready for photographic reproduction.

Clip-out Art – Preprinted art images sold to printers to be cut out and applied directly to artwork.

Coated Papers – Paper made with a fine coat of mineral substance to enhance its printability.

Collating – The gathering of several different items into one organized group.

Color Separation – Photographic process by which a color image is divided into the three primary colors and black film images using filters.

Composition – The typesetting of copy in a selected size and style of type.

Comprehensive – A completed visualization of an image prepared by an artist; final step before preparation of finished art. Sometimes called a *comp*.

Cutting – The separation of larger sheets of paper into smaller ones.

Drilling – The operation of creating round holes in paper or other materials.

Dummy – A folded sample representing a book, booklet or image to be reproduced; used for planning.

Enlarger – A piece of photographic equipment which enlarges images.

Filler Work – Printing jobs taken into the plant, usually at a lower billing rate, to smooth out peaks and valleys of the production schedule.

Flat – Assemblage of film and masking base materials during the image assembly(stripping) phases.

Flat Color – Colors which are specifically mixed to match a sample.

Font – A complete assortment of all characters in one size and series of type.

Form – A collection of images on one plate which will be printed in the same color. – Also called a *printer*.

Freelance Artist – Self-employed person who produces graphic art.

Gathering – see collating.

Grain Direction – The alignment of fibers in a sheet of paper. Long grain being the length and Short grain being the width of a sheet of paper.

Halftone – Reproduction of an image by a pattern of dots of varying sizes and shapes, as related to the light or dark areas of the image.

Ink Coverage – Percentage factor related to the density of ink and the area covered.

Image Assembly – Procedure by which film images are positioned in a precise order for platemaking. Also called *stripping*.

Jogging – The alignment of paper into very even piles to facilitate production.

Labor Intensive – Term describing a condition which requires large numbers of man hours to be spent to obtain a desired result.

Leading – The amount of white space between lines of type.

Lift – A hand held stack of paper to be worked.

Line Copy – Material prepared for reproduction consisting only of high contrast images, lines or dots.

"M" – One thousand.

Mechanical – Artwork which has been fully prepared for reproduction as the first step of a print job.

Moire – An undesirable pattern formed when two or more dotted screen areas are incorrectly overlapped.

Negative – An image on film or paper where the image is clear or white and the background is black.

Numbering Operation – wherein consecutive numbers are printed.

Opaque – Liquid product painted on film with a brush to cover imperfections.

Overlay – Transparent sheets used to separate colors mechanically on art work. Usually one overlay per color.

Padding – Application of adhesive for temporary binding of paper in pads.

Pallet – see Skid.

Paper Caliper – The thickness of paper stock measured in thousandths of inches (or points).

Paste-up – see Mechanical.

Perforated – Small dash cuts made in paper to facilitate tearing.

Pica – A common unit of measurement in typesetting and copy preparation. – One pica equals twelve points and there are approximately 6 picas to an inch.

Ply – Term used to indicate thickness of cardboard. To convert to caliper, multiply the ply value by 3 then add 6 to the results.

PMT – A product manufactured by Kodak and used to go directly from camera to paste-up.

Point(paper) – The equivalent of one thousandth of an inch.

Point (printer's) – Basis for typesetting, where on point equals 1/72 of an inch.

Press-on Type – Letters which are transferred from a master sheet to artwork by pressing or rubbing. – Also called *rub-on* or *transfer* type.

Press Preparation or makeready – The segment of press operation which sets the press up for a particular job to be printed.

Press Running – The continuous operation of a press during which acceptable sheets are being printed for a particular job.

Printing Trade Customs – The operations and business practices held as legal based upon court precedent; usually printed on the reverse side of quotations or proposals.

Process Colors – Specially formulated pigments used in printing process color separations; magenta (red-blue), cyan (blue-green), yellow (red-green) and black as transparent colors. – Often called process red, process blue, process yellow and process black.

Proofing – The visual checking of a job in production.

Registration Marks – Usually appear as two lines in crossed form centered in a circle. Used through out printing production to align (register) images.

Saddle Stitching – The use of wire or other material along the spine (saddle) of gathered signatures, holding them together. Usually one or more staples.

Scored – The creasing of paper stock to provide a line for folding.

Screen Tints – Pieces of film used to divide normally solid areas into design or patterns; two major categories include dots and special effects.

Scribing – The manual removal of film emulsion using a scribing tool or knife. Usually only done to make simple corrections of film images.

Signature – A collection of printed pages on a master sheet, folded in a prearranged sequence to make all or part of a book or booklet.

Skid – Wooden or metal base with runners upon which paper is stacked in large quantities.

Step and Repeat – Procedure by which a single film image is reproduced in a defined manner to provide multiple exact images.

Stripper – Individual who mounts film images into flats to complete image assembly.

Stripping – see Image Assembly.

Thumbnail – Sketches produced by an artist during the initial stages of artwork for a graphic image.

Trimming – The removal of edges or segments of paper stock to bring the final printed product to the desired size.

Uncoated Paper – Paper which does not receive a chemical coating.

Unit Cost – Cost for an individual item or product.

Up – The number of finished sized sheets which can be positioned and printed on a single press run.

Washup – The procedure used for removing ink from a press.

INDEX